Speaking Outside the Courtroom

Speaking Outside the Courtroom

Public Speaking for Lawyers

Henry T. Wihnyk

Senior Legal Skills Professor
University of Florida Levin College of Law

CAROLINA ACADEMIC PRESS
Durham, North Carolina

ISBN. 978-1-5310-0147-6
e-ISBN 978-1-5310-148-3

Library of Congress Cataloging-in-Publication Data

Names: Wihnyk, Henry T., author.
Title: Speaking outside the courtroom : public speaking for lawyers / by
Henry T. Wihnyk.
Description: Durham, North Carolina : Carolina Academic Press, LLC, [2018]
Includes bibliographical references.
Identifiers: LCCN 2018030457 | ISBN 9781531001476 (alk. paper)
Subjects: LCSH: Forensic oratory. | Forensic orations. | Public speaking. |
Communciations in law.
Classification: LCC K181 .W54 2018 | DDC 808.5/102434--dc23
LC record available at https://lccn.loc.gov/2018030457

Carolina Academic Press, LLC
700 Kent Street
Durham, North Carolina 27701
Telephone (919) 489-7486
Fax (919) 493-5668
www.cap-press.com

For Patricia, Claire, Max, Marykate
and Benjamin Maxwell.
You inspire me.

Contents

Acknowledgments   xiii

Introduction   xv

Part One: The Basics   3

1 · Controlling and Surviving Public Speaking Anxiety —
Making the Butterflies Fly in Formation   5

1.1 Accept Anxiety as a Natural Response to Speaking Publically   6

1.2 Strategies for Controlling Public Speaking Anxiety   7

    A. Don't Be Anxious about Being Nervous   7

    B. Square Breathing   8

    C. Act Self-Assured — Convey Confidence   8

    D. Interact with the Audience Members —
       Make Them Your Friends   9

    E. Controlling the Shaky Voice   9

    F. Relieving the Dry Mouth   9

    G. Be Prepared   9

    H. Some Don'ts   9

1.3 Use Public Speaking Anxiety to Your Advantage   10

Sources   10

2 · Know Your Audience   13

2.1 What You Will Need to Know   14

    A. Demographics and Psychological Profile —
       Attitudes, Values, and Beliefs   14

    B. Depth of Knowledge about the Topic   15

    C. Motivation for Attending   15

D. Audience Attitude about the Topic (Chapter 15)   16
E. The Group's "Identity"   17
F. Legislative Bodies   17
2.2 How to Research the Audience   17
A. Interview the Host   17
B. Interview Audience Members   17
C. Use the Internet   17
D. Use a Questionnaire   18
Sources   18

3 · Know Your Speech's Setting and Context, and Control the Logistics 19
Sources   23

4 · Outlining, Organizing, and Crafting Your Speech   25
4.1 How Long Should a Speech Be?   25
4.2 Speech Structure   25
4.3 The Body — Organizational Arrangements for the Body
    of the Speech   27
A. Chronological Arrangement   27
B. Topical Arrangement   28
C. Advantages and Disadvantages Arrangement
    (Compare-Contrast Arrangement)   28
D. Cause and Effect Arrangement   29
E. Spatial Arrangement   30
F. Problem-Solution Arrangement   30
G. Transitions between Points — Connecting the Points   31
4.4 Developing the Main and Supporting Points   32
4.5 Outlining Your Speech   35
Sources   37

5 · Openings and Closings   39
5.1 The Opening   39
A. Gain Audience's Attention and Interest   39
B. Introduce the Topic Clearly and Relate It to the Audience 41
C. Provide a Clear Road Map or Preview to the Speech   42
D. No "Thank you"   42
E. It Goes without Saying   43
5.2 The Closing   43
A. Closing Methods   44
B. The Closing's Structure   45

5.3 Memorize Them   46
Sources   46

6 · Productive Practice Sessions — Practice Makes Permanent   47
  A. Practice Several Times   47
  B. Practice Out Loud   47
  C. Treat Practice Sessions as a Dress Rehearsal   47
  D. Practice with an Audience   48
  E. Record Your Practice Sessions   48
  F. Practice Using Your Notes   48
  G. Practice Using Your Visual Aids   48
Sources   49

Part Two: Delivering the Speech   51

7 · Your Appearance and Demeanor When the Audience
  Isn't the Judge or Jury   53
7.1 Appropriate Attire   53
7.2 Appropriate Attitude and Behavior   54
Sources   60

8 · Using Your Body, Head, and Eyes   61
8.1 Posture and Presence   61
  A. Three-Step Technique for Perfect Posture   61
  B. Convey a Strong Presence   64
8.2 Using Purposeful Movements   66
  A. Transitional Movement Between Points   66
  B. Movement for Emphasis and Dramatic Effect   67
  C. Moving Away from the Audience   68
  D. Point of View Movement (Pro and Con)   68
8.3 Maintaining Eye Contact with the Audience   69
Sources   70

9 · Using Gestures   71
9.1 Purposeful Gesturing   71
9.2 Gestures — What to Use and What to Avoid   72
  A. Gestures to Use   72
  B. Gestures to Avoid   75
9.3 The Ready Position — What to Do When Not Gesturing   81
  A. Effective Ready Positions   81

    B. Ready Positions to Avoid   85
  Sources   92

10 · Using Your Voice   93
  10.1 Vocal Variety   93
  10.2 Vary Purposefully   93
  10.3 Vocal Warmups   95
    A. Articulation Exercises   95
    B. Breathing Exercises   96
  Sources   96

11 · Eliminating Distracting Habits   97
    A. Vocal Fillers   97
    B. "Up-Talking"   98
    C. Distracting Gestures   98
    D. Distracting Movements   99
  Sources   99

12 · Using Your Notes   101
  12.1 The Importance of Using Notes (Don't Memorize)   101
  12.2 Types of Notes and How to Create Them   102
    A. Simple Steps for Preparing Notes   102
    B. Sheet(s) of Paper   102
    C. Note Cards   105
    D. Slideware Programs and Electronic Devices   108
  12.3 Using Notes Correctly — The PG-EC-RS Technique   109
  Sources   110

13 · Using Visual Aids   111
  13.1 Purpose of Visual Aids   111
  13.2 Deciding Whether to Use Visual Aids   111
  13.3 Types of Visual Aids and Techniques for Using Them 112
    A. Objects and Props   112
    B. Handouts   114
    C. Photographs   115
    D. Flip Charts and White Boards   115
    E. Video and Audio   115
    F. Document Camera and Overhead Transparencies   115
    G. Slideware Presentation Programs   115
  13.4 Designing and Using Slideware Presentation Programs 116

A. Slide Design — Composition and Layout   116
B. Slide Presentation   127
Sources   130

Part Three: Types of Speeches   **131**

14 · **The Informative Speech**   **133**
14.1 Organization   133
14.2 Audience Awareness   134
A. Presenting Legal Topics to a Lay Audience   134
B. Presenting Legal Topics to Lawyers   135
14.3 The Importance of Supporting Evidence   135
Sources   136

15 · **The Persuasive Speech**   **137**
15.1 Audience Awareness (Chapter 2)   137
A. Receptive   138
B. Unreceptive (Hostile)   138
C. Neutral   139
D. Combination   139
15.2 Methods (Theories) of Persuasion Outside the Courtroom   140
A. Ethos   140
B. Logos   140
C. Pathos   141
15.3 Format and Organizational Considerations   142
A. Monroe's Motivated Sequence   142
B. Direct Method Arrangement   143
C. Refutation Arrangement   143
15.4 The Importance of Supporting Evidence   143
A. Support Your Points with Examples, Statistics, and Stories   143
B. Cite to the Sources of the Information   144
15.5 Special Considerations for Openings and Closings   144
A. Openings   145
B. Closings   145
Sources   145

16 · **The Question and Answer Session**   **147**
A. Preparing for the Q&A Session   147
B. Conducting the Q&A Session   148
Sources   152

17 · Media Interviews and Press Conferences   153
  17.1 Have a Purpose   153
  17.2 Have a Message   154
  17.3 Prepare   154
    A. Anticipate the Questions   154
    B. Practice   154
  17.4 Answering the Questions during the Interview or
  Press Conference   155
    A. Be Concise   155
    B. Speak to Your Audience   155
    C. Don't Answer What You Don't Know   155
    D. Don't Answer What You Don't Understand   155
    E. Answering Difficult/Hostile Questions   155
  17.5 Expect the Unexpected — The Ambush Interview   156
  17.6 Delivery Techniques for Broadcast Interviews and
  Press Conferences   157
    A. Broadcast Interviews   157
    B. Press Conferences   158
  Sources   158

18 · The Special Occasion Speech   159
  18.1 Types of Special Occasion Speeches   159
  18.2 General Considerations   159
    A. Keep It Short and Sweet   160
    B. It's Not about You   160
    C. Show, Don't Tell   160
    D. Balance Sentiment with Humor, Carefully   160
  18.3 Some Special Delivery Considerations   160
    A. Wedding Toasts   160
    B. The Eulogy   161
  Sources   162

Appendix   163
  Checklists   163
    Part One: The Basics   163
    Part Two: Delivering the Speech   168
    Part Three: Types of Speeches   171

Index   177

Acknowledgments

I am very grateful to:

Kristin B. Gerdy, Teaching Professor and Director of the Rex E. Lee Advocacy Program at the J. Rueben Clark Law School at BYU, for her advice and for generously sharing her teaching materials to help me design my course, Public Speaking for Lawyers.

Dean Laura Rosenbury and Associate Dean Amy Mashburn, who supported my work on this project with a generous research stipend.

My students Jennie Edwards, Ashley Genoese, Kimbrell Hines, Kelly Milliron, Gabriel Roberts, and Michael Sittner, who served as models for this book's illustrations.

Whitney Smith and Donielle Nardi of the law school's Messaging and Ourtreach Department and our talented photographer, Jahi Khalfani, for arranging and taking the photographs used as illustrations in this book.

My brother, Bobby "Patch" Wihnyk, for his insightful comments on drafts of the manuscript.

My wife, Patricia, for her unlimited love, support, and patience while I worked on the manuscript (and all other times as well), and my children, Claire, Max, and Marykate, for putting the "joy" into "the joys of raising a family."

Introduction

You, like the majority of lawyers, will spend a surprisingly small amount of your time in the courtroom. It is more likely that most of your public speaking opportunities will be in non-litigation situations, speaking before governmental bodies, civic and other lay groups, bar organizations, clients and potential clients, the press, and others.

Unfortunately, advocacy training, effective in preparing you for the courtroom, does not provide you with skills needed for public speaking. This is the principal reason why so many lawyers who are virtuosos in the courtroom are inadequate public speakers.

Learning and mastering these skills will be essential to your success as a lawyer. As a skilled public speaker you will be better equipped to represent your clients outside the courtroom. You will be a valued member of your firm, because public speaking events offer excellent opportunities to increase your "visibility" and, therefore, attract clients.

This textbook will guide you in developing and mastering the skills that you'll rely on as a lawyer when engaged in public speaking situations outside the courtroom. Part One walks you through the steps for planning and crafting a speech. In Part Two you'll learn the delivery techniques that will ensure that you get your message across to the audience with style and power. Part Three describes the variety of speeches that you will present to lay and legally trained audiences.

Public speaking is something only learned by doing. Reading this book is only the first step in your journey to become an excellent public speaker. Practice using the techniques and advice offered here. Take every opportunity that you can to speak to audiences. The more you speak, the better you'll become.

Speaking Outside the Courtroom

Part One

The Basics

Chapter 1: Controlling and Surviving Public Speaking Anxiety—
Making the Butterflies Fly in Formation

Chapter 2: Know Your Audience

Chapter 3: Know Your Speech's Setting, Context, and Control the Logistics

Chapter 4: Outlining, Organizing, and Crafting Your Speech

Chapter 5: Openings and Closings

Chapter 6: Productive Practice Sessions—Practice Makes Permanent

Chapter 1

Controlling and Surviving Public Speaking Anxiety— Making the Butterflies Fly in Formation

Anticipation Anxiety

The president of your local bar association telephones and invites you to speak about your state's new family court rules of procedure at the organization's meeting next month. Of course, you accept. As soon as you hang up the phone, however, you regret agreeing to speak. You break out into a sweat. You become anxious every time you think about the event and you put off preparing until the day before you are scheduled to speak.

Presentation Panic

You're sitting on a stage looking out over an audience of people you don't know. You've got butterflies in your stomach, and you feel perspiration trickling down the back of your neck. You hear your name mentioned and the audience applauds. As you stand and walk to the lectern your mouth becomes dry, and your heart races. You stand behind the lectern, trembling and feeling lightheaded. You begin to speak, and your voice is shaky.

Clearly, you are suffering from public speaking anxiety. Join the club!

1.1 Accept Anxiety as a Natural Response to Speaking Publically

Everyone suffers from stage fright in one form or another to one degree or another. It's a natural reaction to the speaking situation. There are many physiological reasons behind this fear. For instance, your body goes into the "fight or flight" mode and produces adrenalin. This is what produces those "butterflies" in your stomach.

But you really don't care about the biology. The bottom line is:

"I'm a lawyer! I shouldn't feel this way!"

Recognize that giving a speech is very different from appearing in court. In the courtroom, you are "on stage," in the comfort zone of playing the role of advocate.

The only thing that matters is that your audience, the jury, understands and believes in your client's case. When speaking publicly outside the courtroom, however, you shed the role of litigator and must appear "as yourself." This is more difficult, because you perceive that the audience is evaluating you "the person."

Self-defeating thoughts crowd your mind placing you under enormous pressure.

I'm a lawyer, so I must be enthralling.

I must be perfect. I can't make a mistake or forget something that I'm supposed to say.

The audience will know that I'm nervous and won't like me.

Clear your mind of these thoughts and practice the following strategies for controlling the anxiety.

1.2 Strategies for Controlling Public Speaking Anxiety

There are no magic ways to eliminate the butterflies, but there are methods to make them fly in formation.

A. Don't Be Anxious about Being Nervous

Or

The only thing we have to fear is fear itself.

It's very common for public speakers to concentrate on the fact that they are nervous and then become anxious about being anxious. This "anxiety sensitivity" creates a vicious circle that magnifies the nervousness. In reality, they are more afraid of being nervous than they are of giving the speech.

Avoid this trap by accepting that you will always be nervous and will always experience the butterflies before you speak. This does not make you unique or demonstrate weakness. These nerves are natural and are suffered by everyone who speaks publically.

Recognize that:

1. You never look as nervous as you feel. Often after speeches, speakers will tell an audience member that they were "so nervous" giving the speech. The audience member will reply honestly that the speaker didn't seem nervous at all. The nerves are internal—you feel them, but the audience doesn't see them.

2. The audience wants you to do well. The audience members are rooting for you and are impressed that you are giving a speech (they are as afraid of public speaking as you are.).

3. The audience is more interested in what you have to say than whether you are nervous.

4. The audience won't be aware of mistakes. When you make a mistake—and you will, because you'll never be perfect—the audience members won't know, because this is the first time they've heard the speech. If you don't react to the mistake, only you will be aware of it.

5. No one is perfect (see above), so don't expect to be. It's okay to make mistakes.

B. Square Breathing

This is a very simple method of calming your nerves. You can do it anywhere and most anytime—even minutes before your speech.

1. Take a slow, deep breath through your nose while you count to four.

2. Hold the breath to the count of four.

3. Release the breath slowly through your mouth to the count of four.

4. Repeat several times.

Breathing slowly and deeply oxygenates your blood, provides energy, sharpens your concentration and your memory, and calms your mind.

C. Act Self-Assured—Convey Confidence

When I was younger I suffered from social anxiety, and I dreaded one-on-one encounters with others. Small talk was physically painful for me. I often became so paralyzed by shyness that I couldn't carry on a conversation. I realized that I needed to do something to ease the anxiety so that I could be successful in business and in my law practice.

I finally came up with a strategy to get me through these situations. Throughout my life, I observed that my brother was very comfortable in social situations. He appeared to be confident, at ease, and to be enjoying socializing. Why couldn't I be more like he was? Well, I decided that at least I could act like he did even if I didn't actually feel as he did. So, when meeting people in small groups in social and business situations, I emulated the way my brother behaved. I smiled, spoke with power, and acted as though I was having fun. At first this was difficult, but I forced myself to attend functions requiring this type of interaction. If I felt as though I couldn't endure the situation and wanted to leave, I forced myself to continue acting confidently.

After some time, it became easier to behave this way. In fact, eventually it felt natural. Gradually, my shyness lessened, and I actually began to enjoy social interaction!

The moral of this story is that even though you are nervous, act self-assured and convey confidence. You'll speak confidently, and eventually, your confidence will be genuine. You'll enjoy speaking to an audience!

A surprising postscript—recently, my brother admitted to me that he too dreaded social situations and suffered with shyness. He appeared to be relaxed and confident because he acted self-assured!

D. Interact with the Audience Members— Make Them Your Friends

Rather than hide backstage or sit silently at the dais, greet audience members as they enter the room. Circulate and mingle with them before you speak. Act confident, be friendly, and give the impression that you are eager to speak.

When you begin to speak, the audience members won't be a group of anonymous faces. You'll have already established a connection that will make you more comfortable.

E. Controlling the Shaky Voice

People often tell me that because they are nervous, their voices sound shaky, especially when they begin to speak. Hearing this makes them even more nervous.

To control this

1. Take a deep breath before you speak. This will give power to your speaking voice.

2. Very briefly clear your throat before you begin to speak.

3. To make your vocal cords "flexible," say a quick "thank you" to the audience as the welcoming applause dies down.

F. Relieving the Dry Mouth

Arrange to have a bottle of water available at the lectern and take sips of the water to hydrate yourself. If you don't have water handy, with your mouth closed, place your tongue flat against the roof of your mouth and push your tongue forward. This will stimulate saliva production.

G. Be Prepared

Practice your speech as often as you can (Chapter 6). The more you practice, the more prepared you'll be. Being prepared will give you confidence.

H. Some Don'ts

1. Don't imagine your audience naked or sitting on the toilet. These visions will terrify you more than giving the speech will.

2. Don't imagine your listeners' heads as rows of cabbages growing in a farm field. You'll lose eye contact, and the listeners will wonder what's so interesting at the back of the room.

3. Don't consume alcohol or take sedatives before the speech to "relax." You may be calm, but you'll also be incoherent. If a cocktail party precedes the speech, drink water, seltzer, or soft drinks. That way you'll be hydrated and sober when you speak.

1.3 Use Public Speaking Anxiety to Your Advantage

Public speaking anxiety requires a lot of energy. The adrenalin coursing through your blood stream is a tremendous source of power. Use that power while you speak. Redirect the desire to pace, shake, rock and gesticulate to your behavior on stage (Chapters 8, 9, and 11). Use the energy to appear confident and enthusiastic.

Sources

Brandin, Dorotea. "How to Embrace Stage Fright and Use it to Your Advantage." Executive Lifestyle, April 22, 2015.

Brown, Heidi K. "Empowering Law Students to Overcome Extreme Public Speaking Anxiety: Why 'Just Be It' Works and 'Just Do It' Doesn't." 53 *Duq. L. Rev.* 181 (2015).

Comm, Joel. "How to Overcome the Fear of Public Speaking in 5 Minutes." Retrieved from https://www.inc.com/joel-comm/7-tips-for-overcoming-your-fear-of-public-speaking.html.

Dempsey, David J. *Legally Speaking: 40 Powerful Presentation Principles Lawyers Need to Know.* New York: Kaplan Publishing, 2009.

Graspy, Ronald P. "Speaking with Confidence." *The Public Speaking Project.* Retrieved from http://publicspeakingproject.org/confidence.html.

Mitchell, Olivia. "The Seven Thinking Sins of Public Speaking." Retrieved from https://speakingaboutpresenting.com/nervousness/thinking-sins-public-speaking/.

Mitchell, Olivia. "The Three Causes of Public Speaking Fear (and what you can do about them)." Retrieved from http://www.speakingaboutpresenting.com/nervousness/fear-of-public-speaking-causes/.

O'Hair, Dan, Hannah Rubenstein, and Rob Stewart. *A Pocket Guide to Public Speaking.* New York: Bedford/St. Martin's, 2016.

Tartakovsky, Margarita. "How to Overcome Being Anxious About Being Anxious." Retrieved from https://psychcentral.com/blog/archives/2012/03/20/how-to-overcome-being-anxious-about-being-anxious/.

Chapter 2

Know Your Audience

Tailor your speech and its delivery to the particular audience you will be addressing. You must know who your listeners will be, what they want and expect from the speech, and how best to deliver your message to them. Therefore, before crafting your speech, you'll need to analyze your prospective audience.

Consider the following two situations:

Episode 1

The local chapter of the chamber of commerce has invited you to speak about issues of interest that the state legislature will address during its upcoming session. Knowing that the organization is made up of local business leaders, you describe pending taxation legislation and its effect on small businesses in the state. The audience members' response to your speech is lukewarm, and during the question and answer period, they ask about legislation related to funding public schools. These questions surprise you, and you are not prepared to answer them.

Episode 2

The local chapter of the chamber of commerce has invited you to speak about issues of interest that the state legislature will address during its upcoming session. You question the person who has invited you to speak to learn about the local chapter's members and the legislative topics that interest them. You view the organization's website and review a list of its legislative priorities. The local chapter supports legislation funding free breakfasts and lunches for all students attending the state's public schools. It has been active in promoting this issue to legislators and community organizations. You realize that the audience members are proud of the work that their chapter has been doing in this regard and will be interested in the effect this initiative has had on the legislature. You ascertain that taxation issues are at the bottom of the organization's list of concerns. You research and craft your speech to focus on the legislation funding public schools. Your audience members are engaged in the presentation.

In Episode 1, you "didn't know your audience." You assumed what it would be like and what it wanted to hear. Your speech was a failure.

In Episode 2, with a little bit of research, you gathered key information about your audience and used it to craft and present a successful speech.

2.1 What You Will Need to Know

Do not assume what your audience will be like. In Episode 1, your speech was not a success, because you guessed that the local business leaders were only interested in taxation issues. You neglected the most important issue of interest. You must research about the audience to find the information.

There are a variety of characteristics that will inform how you craft and deliver your speech.

A. Demographics and Psychological Profile— Attitudes, Values, and Beliefs

1. Age and "Generational Identity"

What is the range or average of audience members' ages? What is the group's generational identity (Generation X, Millennial, Baby Boomers)?

Knowing the average age of your audience will determine how you approach discussing historic events and issues. For example, although JFK's assassination was a significant event in the lives of Baby Boomers, to Millennials, it's merely a chapter in history no more significant than the Lincoln assassination.

It will determine what, if any, cultural references to include in the speech. For example, if you plan to speak to Gen Z (1995–2012) listeners about the portrayal of criminal procedure in movies and television programs, *Law and Order* might be a meaningful example to use. References to *Matlock*, on the other hand, would fall flat.[1]

---

1. I recognize that even this example might be baffling depending on when you're reading this!

2. Gender

Will the audience be a mix of males and females? Does the group cater to one or the other?

3. Income

What is the average income bracket of your audience? What are the ranges of incomes represented?

4. Religion

In many instances, audience members' religious affiliation will affect how you approach certain topics and issues that have the potential of offending them.

5. Political Affiliations

Knowing the audience members' political affiliations is critical if you are presenting a persuasive speech, or if you will be expressing a particular point of view about the subject of an informative speech.

6. Group Affiliations

Members of civic, social, political, community action, and public service organizations share points of views that are of common interest to the particular group. Knowing audience members' affiliations will influence how you approach topics that challenge or affirm the groups' shared attitudes, values, and beliefs.

B. Depth of Knowledge about the Topic

Audience members' familiarity with the topic and knowledge of the related information will drive how you present that information. For example, lay audiences are not familiar with the technicalities involved in legal topics. Legally trained audience members, on the other hand, are familiar with basic legal principles but may not have expertise about all legal topics and processes.

C. Motivation for Attending

1. Voluntary Audience

If your listeners have taken the initiative to attend the speech, it would be safe to assume that they are interested in the topic and are eager to hear you.

In this situation, you still must research your listeners' attributes. Your listeners will attend with the expectation that you are going to be speaking to "them" as they are. If you have not prepared adequately based on audience research, you run the risk of offending your listeners or challenging their attitudes and beliefs, transforming them from eager into hostile listeners.

2. Captive Audience

A captive audience is comprised of listeners who for one reason or another have been required to attend your speech. It is safe to assume that some of these listeners may not want to attend. Although the information that you will provide may ultimately be of interest to them, they will be reluctant to listen, because they are not motivated to hear you speak. Therefore, prepare and present as you would if you were speaking to an unreceptive or neutral audience in a persuasive speech (Chapter 15). It's essential to grab these audience members' attention immediately and to establish common ground with the listeners.

D. Audience Attitude about the Topic (Chapter 15)

Through your research, you need to evaluate the audience's attitude toward you and the speech's topic. There are four categories of audiences that you will address:

1. Receptive

The receptive audience, much like the voluntary audience, is interested in your topic, is eager to listen to you, and agrees with your point of view about the topic.

2. Neutral

The neutral audience is indifferent to or uninformed about the topic. Initially, neutral audience members have little interest in and have not formed opinions about the topic.

3. Unreceptive (Hostile)

This audience does not agree with your point of view about the topic. If you are advocating for a solution to a problem, unreceptive audience members may not agree that the problem exists. They may believe that what you perceive as a problem is, in fact, a favorable situation. If they recognize the problem, they do not agree with the solution that you are promoting.

4. Combination

A combination audience consists of members of all three groups. If you can determine the degree to which each group is represented, it is safe to craft and present the speech aiming at the group composing the largest number of listeners. If, however, you are not certain about how the audience is composed, lean toward crafting and presenting the speech to an unreceptive audience.

E. The Group's "Identity"

If you are addressing the members of an organization, club, or association, research the organization's mission, its positions on public issues, its public service projects, etc.

F. Legislative Bodies

When addressing legislative committees, city councils and county commissions, you will need to gather information about each member. Important information will include the individual's party affiliation, voting record, and public statements about issues related to your topic.

2.2 How to Research the Audience

A. Interview the Host

Many of the questions that you need answered can be addressed by the person inviting you to speak. This person is in the ideal position to describe the audience members' characteristics and attributes. Also, this is the person who can tell you what the group wants to hear and why it wants to hear it.

B. Interview Audience Members

Ask individuals who will be attending your presentation the questions that you've asked the host.

C. Use the Internet

Most organizations, civic groups, condominium associates and other groups have websites that provide a wealth of information. You'll also discover news articles and other postings revealing helpful information about the audience.

D. Use a Questionnaire

Provide a questionnaire to prospective audience members asking for information that will help you craft and deliver a speech that is relevant to them.

Sources

Decaro, Peter. "Audience Analysis." *The Public Speaking Project.* Retrieved from http://publicspeakingproject.org/psvirtualtext.html.

Dempsey, David J. *Legally Speaking: 40 Powerful Presentation Principles Lawyers Need to Know.* New York: Kaplan Publishing, 2009.

O'Hair, Dan, Hannah Rubenstein, and Rob Stewart. *A Pocket Guide to Public Speaking.* New York: Bedford/St. Martin's, 2016.

Chapter 3

Know Your Speech's Setting and Context, and Control the Logistics

In addition to knowing your audience, it is vital that you have information about the setting, context, and logistics for your presentation. The venue's conditions and equipment will influence how you draft and present your speech. Gather this information well in advance of the event. The first time you learn these details should not be when you arrive at the venue. Unexpected conditions and the absence of necessary equipment can spoil your presentation.

Ask your host to arrange the venue and to provide necessary equipment. If the host is not able to, then be prepared to handle these arrangements yourself. Visit the venue in advance of your performance so that you will have firsthand knowledge about the conditions. Practice using the visual aid equipment that your host provides. This is especially important to ensure that your operation of slideware and video equipment will be smooth and professional.

The following is a list of many, but not necessarily all, of the questions you should address to gather the information you'll need to plan and present a successful speech.

1. When and where will you be speaking?

As it gets closer to the day of the event, verify the date, time, and location. Strange things happen. The host may have made schedule changes and neglected to notify you.

2. How long will you be permitted to speak?

As with location and date, this is information that you should verify as the event approaches.

3. What is the size of the room and the audience? and How will audience seating be arranged?

Knowing this information in advance will help you determine details such as

- How you can and should move on stage;

- How to maintain eye contact with audience members;

- Whether you'll need to amplify your voice; and

- What kind of visual aids will be practical.

4. Will you be standing on the floor at audience level, on a slightly raised platform, or on a stage?

This information will be important to you for planning, practicing, and executing your movements during the speech.

- At floor/audience level you will be able to move close to the audience for dramatic effect (Chapter 8). On the other hand, at floor level, there is a risk that audience members in the back of the room may have difficulty seeing you and your visual aids.

- Depending on its height, a slightly raised platform will improve your visibility to audience members. If the platform is placed close to the audience, you can still use movement for dramatic effect. Be aware of the platform's size to avoid walking off its edge.

- A stage's advantage is that it puts you and your visual aids in full view of the audience. The downside is that standing on a stage places a physical and psychological distance between you and your audience.

5. Will you be illuminated by ambient lighting or by stage lighting?

- In dim lighting, it may be difficult for audience members to see you and visual aids such as objects and photographs.

- Projections on a screen can be "washed out" if the lighting is too bright.

- Stage lighting can cause "spotlight blindness," keeping you from seeing nearly everyone in the audience (Chapter 8).

6. Will a lectern be available and where will it be located on stage?

- How will it affect your visibility, movements, and visual aids?

- Can it be removed if you prefer not to use it?

- Is it designed to accommodate your notes? Will the work surface be large enough for you to conveniently place sheets of paper or note cards?

- How tall is it? Will it be too short to be practical, or so tall that it will hide you from view?

7. Will you require and be supplied with a microphone?

- If the room's acoustics are unsatisfactory, ask your host to provide a microphone.

- Will the microphone be stationary or portable?

  Some microphones are fixed to the lectern and can't be moved. This will limit your movement about the stage.

- If portable, will it be wireless?

  Wireless microphones provide the flexibility for you to move about the stage. They often malfunction, however, so test the equipment before the speech.

  Hand-held microphones are "portable" in the sense that you can carry them as you move about the stage. On the down side, holding them limits your ability to gesture.

8. Will equipment designed for displaying visual aids be available?

- Arrange for your host to provide the equipment you need. This may include an easel, white board, computer, projector and screen, video and audio equipment.

- Will the equipment be compatible with your slideware program files?

- Arrange for the opportunity to test and practice with the equipment before your performance.

- If equipment will not be available, will the room be outfitted to accommodate your own equipment? You will need a power source and extension cords for your computer and projector. Also, you will require sufficient room for placing and using your equipment.

- Will you use a remote control or will you need a person's assistance to operate the equipment? Examine and practice with the remote before your performance. Consult and practice with the person who will be assisting you.

9. Who will handle arrangements for handouts?

- Will you or your host print and duplicate handout materials?

- Will you or your host pay for printing and duplicating handouts?

10. Will audience members have the opportunity to ask you questions?

- Inform the host that you prefer not to take questions during your speech but will conduct a Q&A session immediately following the presentation (Chapter 16).

- Will audience members need amplification to ask questions?

  If the room and audience are large, it may be necessary to set up microphones for audience questions. Discourage your host from providing only handheld microphones that audience members must pass around.

11. Who will introduce you?

- Obtain contact details so that you can provide that person with the information you want included in the introduction.

12. Will others speak before or after you speak?

- If so, who will they be and what topics will they address?

  You will need to know the other speakers' topics, so that you can adjust your speech accordingly. Usually an event with several speakers revolves around a central theme. Without planning, this can lead to speakers duplicating topics and content. Obtain contact details so that you can consult with the other speakers. It's safer to obtain the information from the speakers themselves rather than merely to rely on your host.

13. Will a meal be served at the event and, if so, will it be served before, during, or after you speak?

- If you are speaking before a meal is served, expect distractions caused by the wait staff setting up for the meal. Also, expect that audience members may be impatient about eating.

- If you are speaking during the meal, you can expect that the room will be noisy and that you'll be fighting with servers and the meal itself for attention. It's difficult for people to eat in silence, so audience members will talk with each other while you are speaking.

- The optimum time to speak is after the meal is served and the tables have been cleared. Audience members will be relaxed and will be able to give you their full attention. Speak with energy, because your listeners may be drowsy after eating.

14. Will you or your host handle your hotel and travel arrangements?

Don't take for granted that the host will make the arrangements. Finding out at the last minute that it was up to you can leave you without a way to travel to the event and without a place to stay. If the host will handle the travel and hotel details, be very specific about your travel and accommodation needs and preferences.

15. Will you or your host pay for your travel and hotel expenses?

Don't be afraid to ask about this. Although it will be clear very early whether your host will pay for your travel, you may not discover that you must pay for your hotel room until you've arrived, or worse, when you are checking out.

Sources

Dempsey, David J. *Legally Speaking: 40 Powerful Presentation Principles Lawyers Need to Know*. New York: Kaplan Publishing, 2009.

Detz, Joan. *It's Not What You Say, It's How You Say It*. New York: St. Martins Griffin, 2000.

Chapter 4

Outlining, Organizing, and Crafting Your Speech

4.1 How Long Should a Speech Be?

When asked how long a person's legs should be, Abraham Lincoln replied, "Long enough to reach from the body to the ground." Like a person's legs, a speech should be only as long as it needs to be, with some limits.

Your speech should be long enough to provide information without boring your listeners. Be sensitive to your audience members' attention spans. Although experts disagree about the length of the average person's attention span, it's safe to assume that your audience members' attention will wander after about ten minutes. Therefore, strive to craft speeches to be no longer than that. If it's necessary for you to speak longer, incorporate topic changes or other devices to regain attention.

4.2 Speech Structure

The large-scale organization (outline) of most speeches is standard and contains the following elements:

- Opening

- Body

- Closing

─────────── Basic Outline of a Speech ───────────

Opening (**Chapter 5**)

    • Gain attention.

    • State the central idea.

    • Provide a roadmap of main points.

– Transition –

Body

        Main Point 1

            A. Support

            B. Support

            C. Support

– Transition –

        Main Point 2

            A. Support

            B. Support

            C. Support

– Transition –

        Main Point 3

            A. Support

            B. Support

            C. Support

– Transition –
(Signal that the speech is concluding.)

Closing (**Chapter 5**)

    • Restate the central idea.

    • Summarize the main points.

    • Close

4.3 The Body—Organizational Arrangements for the Body of the Speech

There are a variety of arrangements that you can use to organize the main points in the body of the speech. The style you use will depend on the speech's subject and purpose. In addition to these arrangements, there are special considerations related to persuasive speaking (Chapter 15).

A. Chronological Arrangement

This arrangement is useful when describing a sequence of events or steps in a process. This is the arrangement most often used in informative speeches about current or historical events, life stories, and in demonstrations. It's the typical way to tell a story.

For Example:

• **Sequence of Events**
The Rotary Club invited you to speak at its luncheon meeting about a recent product liability case that you tried against the manufacturer of a pressure cooker.

> *Central Idea: A manufacturer's failure to heed the warnings about its product's faulty design leads to a large punitive damages verdict.*

> *Main Point 1—The Accident*
> *Your client loses her right hand when a pressure cooker she's using explodes.*

> *Main Point 2—The Investigation*
> *During discovery, you find memoranda written by the defendant's research and development department that warns about a faulty valve design that could cause explosions when the product is used.*

> *Main Point 3—The Trial and Verdict*
> *The defendant's president admits that he approved marketing the product despite the warnings, and the jury awards punitive damages.*

• **Steps in a Process**
You are speaking at the local library as part of the "Know Your Rights" series open to the public. Your topic, "Pursuing a Small Claims Case."

Central Idea: Prosecuting a small claims case is a relatively simple process for obtaining redress in the courts.

Main Point 1 — Write a complaint and file it in the small claims court clerk's office.

Main Point 2 — Gather evidence and select witnesses that you will present during the trial.

Main Point 3 — Present your evidence and witnesses in court.

B. Topical Arrangement

Use this arrangement for complicated topics that involve several independent points. Although independent, the points work together to support the central idea. It's important that your transitions emphasize how the points are connected.

For example:

You are speaking about estate planning at a condominium association. You have been asked to explain the different planning methods.

Central Idea: There are several methods that you can use to ensure that your family is protected, and that your property is distributed according to your wishes after you die.

Main Point 1 — Wills are a way to ensure that, during probate, your property is distributed according to your wishes.

Main Point 2 — Living trusts are a way to avoid probate and establish a plan for your assets.

Main Point 3 — Life insurance policies provide cash to cover your funeral expenses and debts and provide support for your dependents.

Each point focuses on a different method, but each method is an example of the central idea.

C. Advantages and Disadvantages Arrangement (Compare-Contrast Arrangement)

This arrangement allows you to show how two or more things are similar or different. This is useful for both informing and persuading your audience.

This arrangement is useful in a persuasive speech for demonstrating the risks and benefits of a particular solution to a problem. In the Advantages and Disadvantages Arrangement, you might examine competing solutions or positions about an issue, setting out the positives and negatives of each and defending one. You can also use it in an informative speech when describing a particular action or solution.

For Example:

> *You are speaking to members of a condominium association about estate planning. You are describing the differences between wills and living trusts and advising which is the best method.*
>
> > *Central Idea: Wills and living trusts, each with their own advantages and disadvantages, provide different ways to control how your property is distributed to your beneficiaries.*
> >
> > *Main Point 1 — Wills must go through a lengthy probate process in order to take effect but are relatively inexpensive.*
> >
> > *Main Point 2 — Living trusts avoid the probate process and the involvement of courts but are more costly to create and manage.*
> >
> > *Main Point 3 — Wills become public record at the time of your death, but living trusts remain private.*

D. Cause and Effect Arrangement

In this arrangement, the speaker identifies a certain situation (cause) and then describes the response (effect). This arrangement works well for informative speeches.

For example:

> *You are speaking at a meeting of the local bar association about a new rule affecting attorneys serving on local professionalism panels.*
>
> > *Central Idea: Lawsuits against attorneys for acts performed while serving on local professionalism panels have resulted in the state supreme court adopting a new rule providing immunity from civil liability.*
> >
> > *Main Point 1 — Many attorneys serving on local professionalism panels that resolve complaints of unprofessional conduct by attorneys have been subject to civil liability for acts performed in the course of their duties on panels. Therefore, the state bar association hasn't been able to recruit enough attorneys to serve on the panels. (Cause)*

Main Point 2—The state's supreme court has amended the Code for Resolving Professionalism Complaints to provide absolute immunity from civil liability to attorneys serving on professionalism panels for all acts performed in the course and scope of their duties on the panels. (Effect)

E. Spatial Arrangement

Use this arrangement when you are describing the configuration of the parts or levels of a structure, place, system, or object. Arrange the main points so that they represent how the parts relate to each other.

For example:

You are speaking to high school students about the state's court system.

Central Idea: Our state's court system is comprised of three levels, each providing specialized judicial services.

Main Point1—The state supreme court is the highest level court. It decides cases emanating from the appellate courts that raise issues of great public importance.

Main Point 2—The state appellate courts are the intermediate level courts. They decide appeals from trial court decisions.

Main Point 3—The state trial courts are the lowest level courts. They are where criminal matters and disputes between citizens are litigated.

F. Problem-Solution Arrangement

This arrangement is most often used in persuasive speeches when the speaker wants the audience to take a particular action. First you identify and describe the problem and its causes. Next, you propose a solution to the problem and convince the audience to accept or apply the solution.

For example:

You are speaking at a city council meeting where you are attempting to convince the council to approve a particular ordinance.

Central Idea: An ordinance requiring landlords to perform criminal background checks of prospective tenants will reduce the rate of violent crimes in the city.

Main Point 1—Violent crime in our city has increased by 25% over the past two years, because dangerous criminals have been moving here.

Main Point 2—Preventing these criminals from renting apartments in the town will decrease the number of criminals moving to our city.

Main Point 3—To protect, preserve, and promote the health, safety, welfare, peace, and quiet of the citizens of our city, the city commission should approve Article 14 of the City Ordinances requiring landlords to perform criminal background checks of prospective tenants.

G. Transitions between Points— Connecting the Points

Transitions make your speech coherent. As you move from point to point, guide your audience with transitions that show the relationships between the points.

When linking the points and moving from one point to the next, transitions serve several specific purposes:

- They signal that the speaker is moving from the introduction to the body of the speech.

    "First"

    "First thing to remember"

    "To begin with"

- They show a progression from one point to the next.

    "Then"

    "Next"

    "Additionally"

    "In addition"

    "First, second, third"

- They link sections that demonstrate contrasting or similar points.

    "Although this may be true"

    "At the same time"

> *"Conversely"*
>
> *"On the other hand"*
>
> *"However"*

- They link points demonstrating cause and effect.

> *"As a result"*
>
> *"Consequently"*
>
> *"Then"*

- They signal that the speaker is moving from the body of the speech to the conclusion.

> *"In summary"*
>
> *"In conclusion"*
>
> *"To sum up"*

4.4 Developing the Main and Supporting Points

Three Main Points

Studies reveal that people can digest and remember information best in clumps of three. Their ability to digest and remember information, however, decreases as the amount of information increases.

Also, they can take in only a limited amount of information without losing interest. If you craft your speech with too many main points, you'll make it difficult for your audience. Don't make your audience work while listening to you.

Imagine that you are in an audience listening to a speech about new trends in a particular area of law. In the opening, the speaker previews the speech's body by telling you that she'll be covering fourteen topics. Your reaction would be to think that "oh my, this is going to go on forever." You'll look for the nearest exit. Certainly, you won't be an eager listener.

On the other hand, imagine that the speaker tells the audience that she'll be covering three topics. Your reaction will be to sit back, relax and listen.

It is essential, therefore, to limit the number of points that you cover during the speech—preferably to three. This doesn't mean, however, that you can't cover more than three bits of information. If your central idea covers more than three points, do your best to condense them by grouping them into categories.

For example, assume that you are speaking to members of the local affiliate of the National Education Association about the state's statutory principles of professional conduct relating to a teacher's obligations to students. These obligations are listed as follows:

Obligation to the student requires that the teacher:

1. Shall make reasonable effort to protect the student from conditions harmful to learning and/or to the student's mental and/or physical health and/or safety.

2. Shall not unreasonably restrain a student from independent action in pursuit of learning.

3. Shall not unreasonably deny a student access to diverse points of view.

4. Shall not intentionally suppress or distort subject matter relevant to a student's academic program.

5. Shall not intentionally expose a student to unnecessary embarrassment or disparagement.

6. Shall not intentionally violate or deny a student's legal rights.

7. Shall not harass or discriminate against any student on the basis of race, color, religion, sex, age, national or ethnic origin, political beliefs, marital status, handicapping condition, sexual orientation, or social and family background and shall make reasonable efforts to assure that each student is protected from harassment or discrimination.

8. Shall not exploit a relationship with a student for personal gain or advantage.

9. Shall keep in confidence personally identifiable information obtained in the course of professional service, unless disclosure serves professional purposes or is required by law.[2]

Presenting these as nine separate main points would be unwieldy and difficult for your audience to absorb. However, by categorizing the obligations, you'd make the information easier for you to cover and easier for your audience to digest.

---

2. Rule 5A-10.081 of the Florida Administrative Code.

For example:

1. *Obligation to protect students' rights to an education*

    A. Shall make reasonable effort to protect the student from conditions harmful to learning and/or to the student's mental and/or physical health and/or safety.

    B. Shall not unreasonably restrain a student from independent action in pursuit of learning.

    C. Shall not unreasonably deny a student access to diverse points of view.

    D. Shall not intentionally suppress or distort subject matter relevant to a student's academic program.

2. *Obligation to protect students' individual rights*

    A. Shall not intentionally expose a student to unnecessary embarrassment or disparagement.

    B. Shall not intentionally violate or deny a student's legal rights.

    C. Shall not harass or discriminate against any student on the basis of race, color, religion, sex, age, national or ethnic origin, political beliefs, marital status, handicapping condition, sexual orientation, or social and family background and shall make reasonable effort to assure that each student is protected from harassment or discrimination.

3. *Obligation to maintain a professional relationship with students*

    A. Shall not exploit a relationship with a student for personal gain or advantage.

    B. Shall keep in confidence personally identifiable information obtained in the course of professional service, unless disclosure serves professional purposes or is required by law.

Thus, you've condensed nine items into three main points. The nine items become the supporting points for the main points. You could condense some of the supporting points to add additional streamlining.

4.5 Outlining Your Speech

You've selected your topic and you are ready to write the speech. First, just as with writing an essay, it's important to prepare an outline of the speech.

This doesn't mean that you must follow the formal rules for outlining. Worrying about the formal structure of an outline will inhibit your ability to develop your ideas. Instead, start with a non-linear outline. This will encourage creativity in developing your main points, supporting points and in determining the order in which you'll present them.

First, brainstorm about the main points and supporting points. Write down your ideas for main points anywhere on the page and circle them. As you brainstorm, you'll think of supporting points for these main points. As you do, place the supporting point in a circle branching out from the relevant main point. Do this for all the points. Then number the main points in the order that you'll speak about them. Finally, use letters to indicate the order in which you will discuss the supporting points. You can use this outline to write the speech or convert this into a formal outline before drafting the speech.

For example, you are preparing a speech about injunctions for protection against domestic violence. You brainstorm about what you intend to discuss. One main point is how to obtain the injunction—write that down and circle it. Supporting points will be preparing pleadings, getting a temporary injunction, and having a hearing. Another main point that comes to mind covers actions that can be taken after obtaining an injunction. Supporting points will be extending the injunction, modifying the injunction, and dissolving the injunction. Next, you decide to discuss enforcing an injunction as a main point. The involvement of police, the court, and the state attorney will be supporting points. Finally, you decide the order in which you'll discuss the points. First will be obtaining the injunction (Label it 1). Next you'll discuss enforcing the injunction (Label it 2). Finally you'll discuss what can be done after the injunction is obtained (Label it 3). Then label the supporting points with letters to indicate the order in which you will discuss each. The final non-linear outline will look like Figure 4.5-a.

Once you've finished the non-linear outline, you can convert it into a more formal outline.

Figure 4.5-a Non-Linear Outline

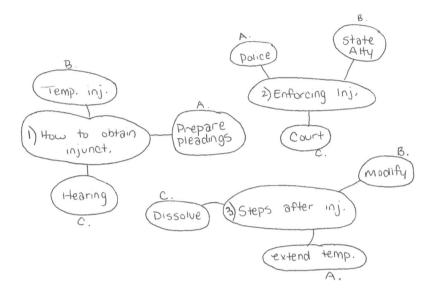

I. How to obtain an injunction against domestic violence.

   A. How to prepare a petition for an injunction against domestic violence.

   B. Obtaining a temporary injunction while waiting for a court hearing.

   C. What to expect at the hearing to determine whether the court will enter a permanent injunction.

II. How to enforce a permanent injunction against domestic violence.

   A. The role law enforcement officers play when enforcing the injunction.

   B. The role the state attorney will play if the injunction is violated.

   C. The role the court will play when enforcing the injunction.

III. Actions to take after the court enters an injunction.

   A. How to obtain an order extending a temporary injunction.

   B. How to obtain an order modifying the terms of the injunction.

C. How to obtain an order dissolving an injunction.

Once you have a skeleton of what you plan to say, transform the working outline into the speech. Use what you've written and outlined to craft your speaking notes.

Sources

Barnett, Joshua Trey. "Organizing and Outlining." *The Public Speaking Project.* Retrieved from http://publicspeakingproject.org/psvirtualtext.html.

Dempsey, David J. *Legally Speaking: 40 Powerful Presentation Principles Lawyers Need to Know.* New York: Kaplan Publishing, 2009.

O'Hair, Dan, Hannah Rubenstein, and Rob Stewart. *A Pocket Guide to Public Speaking.* New York: Bedford/St. Martin's, 2016.

Chapter 5

Openings and Closings

5.1 The Opening

"You never get a second chance to make a first impression."
Will Rogers

The quality of your opening can determine your speech's success. It determines whether and how your audience will listen to you.

If the speech is to be successful, the introduction must gain the audience's attention and interest, clearly identify the topic and relate it to the audience, and provide a road map or preview of the speech's content.

A. Gain Audience's Attention and Interest

Regardless of the type of speech that you are giving, you must immediately grab your audience's attention. If you are presenting a continuing education course to other lawyers, you can imagine that they are expecting to be bored by a "lesson." If you are presenting to a lay audience, the audience members may be apprehensive because they won't understand the topic or because they will be bored by dry, technical legal information. Capturing your audience's attention will shift its attitude to being receptive to your message.

There are several ways to gain the audience's attention. Choose and use the method that is appropriate for the speech topic and its context and that fits with your personality.

1. Surprising Statistic

This is a statistic that relates to your topic and is not generally known to the audience. It should be relevant and accurate. Cite to the source. For example, in a speech about the dangers of high-speed pursuits:

> *"According to the Bureau of Justice Statistics, from 1996 to 2015, an average of 355 persons (about 1 per day) were killed annually in pursuit-related crashes."*

2. A Shocking Statement

Be sure that the statement is relevant, accurate, and believable. This can be combined with the surprising statistic. For example, in a speech about the Madoff investment scandal:

> *"Bernie Madoff defrauded 4,800 of his clients out of 64.8 billion dollars."*

3. Quotation

The quotation should be relevant and interesting. It's best that the quote be by a known person. The Will Rogers quote at the beginning of this chapter is a good example.

Be careful, however, not to use a quotation that is so well known and overused that it is a cliché.

4. Rhetorical Question or Survey Question

When you use a rhetorical question in the opening, you aren't really seeking an answer. It's a provocative way to make a point and to get the audience thinking.

> *"Did you expect the judge to do anything else?"*

> *"Could the client be any less cooperative?"*

> *"Could the statute be any more confusing?"*

Unlike the rhetorical question, a survey question seeks an answer. If performed effectively, a survey question does a good job of relating the topic to the audience. This can be awkward, however, if the audience does not respond to the question. If you ask such a question, be sure to relate the answer to the topic.

> *"How many of you know …"*

> *"How many of you have …"*

5. An Enthralling Story

Research by psychologists demonstrates that our brains become more active when we listen to stories. Therefore, stories help engage and persuade listeners.

Use stories at the speech's opening, but keep them short, simple, and related to the speech's topic and theme.

6. Humor

It takes a very good joke to be better than no joke at all. Humor can be effective, but it is very risky. There is always the danger that audience members will not get the joke or will be offended by it. In either case, you'll be starting the speech in a very awkward position.

Only use humor if you have vetted the joke with others so that you know that your audience will appreciate it. Be sure that the joke is related to the speech's topic. Finally, be sure that you can tell the joke well.

Self-deprecating humor can work if the audience knows you. If you are addressing a lay audience, however, be careful not to appear silly. A lay audience expects a lawyer to be mature, professional, and self-assured. You want the audience members to have confidence in you and the information that you are providing. A joke can impair that.

7. A Visual or Audio Aid (Chapter 13)

As with stories, audiences are drawn in by interesting visual aids. A video or sound recording can be a dramatic way to begin.

Be careful here, because any awkwardness manipulating the visual aid will destroy the opening's impact and, therefore, will diminish the speech's effectiveness.

Regardless of the technique you use:

- Be genuine.
- Do not be overly dramatic.
- Do not behave in a shocking manner or "out of character" for the speech's context.
- Do not say that you are nervous, inexperienced, or unprepared.

B. Introduce the Topic Clearly and Relate It to the Audience

Let the audience know what you'll be talking about even though the topic has been advertised and mentioned by the person introducing you. Briefly refer to how or why the topic is important and relevant to the audience. It could be as simple as indicating that the audience has expressed interest in the topic. In some cases, gaining the audience's attention will serve this purpose.

C. Provide a Clear Road Map or Preview to the Speech

Your audience should know what to expect. It will be better able to follow the speech if you explain what topics or points the speech will cover in the order in which you'll cover them.

It shouldn't be a mechanical rendition of the topics:

> *"I will tell you about the elements of a contract. First, I'll talk about the offer. Next, I will explain consideration. Finally, I will tell you about performance."*

Not only is this dull, it directs the audience's focus on you rather than the topic.

A stronger road map is more subtle than that. It provides a preview and directs the audience's attention to the speech's theme and topics:

> *"There are three elements that are necessary for a contract. There must be an offer, there must be consideration and there must be performance."*

Provide the road map but don't take the audience on the trip in the introduction.

> *"There are three elements that are required for an enforceable contract. First, there must be an offer. <u>An offer is when a person makes a promise to do something when</u>…. There must be consideration. <u>Consideration is</u>…. Finally, there must be performance <u>which involves</u>…."*

The road map should be concise. Wait until the speech's body to go into detail about your topics or points.

D. No "Thank you"

If you have been invited to speak to members of an organization, do not spend your time thanking the organization's officers, the individuals who have organized the event, or the individuals who invited you to speak. The audience is not interested in hearing you thank these people, and the people will not be offended if you don't mention them. Obviously you appreciate their inviting you. Thank them privately before or after the presentation.

If you must acknowledge important individuals, keep it to ten seconds. Avoid saying, "I want to thank Bob Wilson for inviting me." If you want to thank Bob, then thank him. Instead, say, "Thank you, Bob, for inviting me," or "Bob Wilson, thank you for inviting me."

That said, feel free to thank, very briefly, the person who introduces you to the audience. Don't, however, gush over the introduction's content.

"Thank you, Bob."

Not

"Thank you, Bob for that wonderful introduction. It was kind of you to say all those nice things about me...."

E. It Goes without Saying

Don't spend time introducing yourself. The host will have introduced you and described your background and qualifications. The audience knows who you are and will consider references to these things as merely boasting.

Bottom line—get right to the speech.

5.2 The Closing

The speech's closing should be as powerful and vivid as the opening. Use the closing to leave the audience with a positive impression about you and the speech. Just as the opening establishes the audience members' first impression about the speech, the closing leaves them with the concluding impression that they will take with them and remember. Think about how you feel when you are leaving a movie theater after watching a film that has a moving, powerful conclusion. You leave with a much more positive impression than when the film ends with a whimper. That's how you want your audience to feel after you've spoken.

There are several effective techniques that you can use to close the speech.

A. Closing Methods

1. Bookend Closing

As you close, refer back to something you said in the introduction. For example, assume that in your introduction you say,

"The Scopes trial put evolution in the spotlight."

When you close you say:

"The spotlight on evolution resulting from the Scopes trial has illuminated the conflict between religion and science."

2. Challenge Closing

This technique should always be used as a call to action in a persuasive speech. Once you've convinced the audience members about your point of view during the speech, close by urging them to apply what they've been told. For example:

"Approve the ordinance and fix our city's streets."

"Vote against this bill to preserve our citizens' water rights."

"Write Senator Spurber and tell her to confirm Judge Matterly."

3. Echo Closing

Repeat a word from a quotation relating it to the call to action.

"'Have a dream' that one day our town's children will...."

"They 'can fool' some on the board 'some of the time,' and some of the board 'all the time,' but they 'cannot fool' the entire board 'all the time.'"

4. Repetitive Closing

Repeat a word or phrase several times for dramatic effect.

"Justice for the poor. Justice for the wealthy. Justice for us all."

5. Callback Closing

Refer back to the story mentioned in the opening.

"Recall the story I told you about Mary and her struggle with drugs? Well, the court gave Mary a second chance by sending her to Success House,

and today she is employed, married, the mother of three, and most importantly, drug free."

6. Quotation Closing

Conclude with a short, famous quotation or line from a poem. Pause before you recite the quotation and provide attribution.

"I think Yogi Berra was right when he said, 'You got to be careful if you don't know where you're going, because you might not get there.'"

"As Sir Winston Churchill told us, 'Sometimes it is not enough that we do our best; we must do what is required.'"

Ronald Reagan eloquently concluded his address to the nation about the explosion of the space shuttle Challenger by seamlessly incorporating lines from John Gillespie Magee's poem "High Flight."

"The crew of the space shuttle Challenger honored us by the manner in which they lived their lives. We will never forget them, nor the last time we saw them, this morning, as they prepared for their journey and waved goodbye and 'slipped the surly bonds of earth' to 'touch the face of God.'"

Aim for a vivid closing. It isn't necessary, however, to be flamboyant and overly dramatic.

B. The Closing's Structure

Regardless of which of these techniques you use, include the following in the closing:

1. Signal

Provide a transition (Chapter 4) that signals that you are moving from the body of the speech to the closing. For example:

"In closing"

"In conclusion"

"Finally"

It is important that audience members are aware that you are wrapping up. Otherwise they will be confused, thinking that you are still in the body of the speech. This will result in the closing being abrupt and ineffective.

2. Summary

Smoothly provide a brief summary of the main points and reinforce the speech's theme.

> *"As you can see, each part of a contract, the offer, acceptance, consideration, and performance can be the subject of legal disputes."*

Avoid a stilted listing of the topics and the theme such as:

> *"First, we covered the offer and acceptance, then I told you about consideration, and then I described performance. Then I told you about how each of these can cause legal disputes."*

> *"I hope you have learned about the parts of a contract."*

> *"I hope you understand…."*

After you close, stay on stage and bask in the applause. Don't rush off.

5.3 Memorize Them

The opening must grab your audience's attention and interest. The closing must leave your audience with a positive lasting impression. To achieve this, you must maintain constant eye contact with the audience, and avoid glancing at notes. You must have complete confidence in what you are saying and speak without any hesitation. Unlike the rest of the speech, therefore, these two portions must be memorized to guarantee that you present them powerfully.

Sources

Dempsey, David J. *Legally Speaking: 40 Powerful Presentation Principles Lawyers Need to Know.* New York: Kaplan Publishing, 2009.

O'Hair, Dan, Hannah Rubenstein, and Rob Stewart. *A Pocket Guide to Public Speaking.* New York: Bedford/St. Martin's, 2016.

Smith, Jacquelyn. "7 Excellent Ways to Start a Presentation and Capture Your Audience's Attention." Retrieved from http://business.financialpost.com/business-insider/7-excellent-ways-to-start-a-presentation-and-capture-your-audiences-attention.

Chapter 6

Productive Practice Sessions— Practice Makes Permanent

A. Practice Several Times

Once is not enough! Practice your speech enough times that it becomes second nature to you. Do not memorize it, but know it so well that you could, if necessary, present it without your notes.

B. Practice Out Loud

This piece of advice isn't as obvious as it might seem. I've asked students who did not present an effective speech whether they practiced.

"Oh yes. I went over it in my head several times."

"You didn't practice out loud?"

"No."

The first time you say the words shouldn't be when you are in front of the audience!

C. Treat Practice Sessions as a Dress Rehearsal

Practice makes permanent. The way you practice will become the way you present the speech. Therefore, treat every practice session as a "dress rehearsal." That means you should practice "in character," behaving and appearing as you will during the actual presentation. If you make a mistake, don't stop. Continue on so that you will get experience "covering" mistakes during the speech.

Use the practice sessions to plan and practice purposeful gestures and movements. Use the practice session to time your speech and cut it if it's too long.

Practice under conditions similar to those you'll encounter at the time of your presentation. If possible, practice in the location where you'll be speaking.

D. Practice with an Audience

A speech isn't a solitary, isolated activity—you won't be speaking to an empty room. Therefore, just as the actual presentation shouldn't be the first time you say the words, the actual presentation shouldn't be the first time an audience hears them. Your speech's success depends, in large part, on how you and the audience connect. When practicing with an audience (even if there are only one or two people), you'll get an actual sense of how you and the speech will be received, and you'll get helpful feedback.

E. Record Your Practice Sessions

It is essential that you record and view your practice sessions to evaluate and perfect your delivery. A recording shows how the audience will see and hear you. It shows how you really look, how you really sound, and it catches every movement and gesture, strong as well as weak.

Use the recordings to evaluate your speech's organization and content in addition to your delivery. The speech may look good on paper and may sound great to you while you practice, but how does it come across to your audience? The recording will allow you to put yourself in the audience's position and objectively ascertain whether the speech conveys your message. Also, it will permit you to objectively evaluate your visual aids' effectiveness.

F. Practice Using Your Notes

It's important to become comfortable manipulating and reading your notes while you speak. Use the practice sessions to evaluate whether the note system you've chosen works as you need it to, and to assess whether you've crafted the notes so that you can read them easily at a glance.

G. Practice Using Your Visual Aids

Practice with the actual visual aids you plan to use exactly as you plan to incorporate them into your performance. This is essential if you will be using slideware, video, or audio. Practice with the equipment you'll be using during your presentation. If possible, arrange to practice at the venue where you'll be speaking, especially if you will be using the host's equipment. This is essential if you will be using the host's equipment.

Sources

Dempsey, David J. *Legally Speaking: 40 Powerful Presentation Principles Lawyers Need to Know*. New York: Kaplan Publishing, 2009.

O'Hair, Dan, Hannah Rubenstein, and Rob Stewart. *A Pocket Guide to Public Speaking*. New York: Bedford/St. Martin's, 2016.

Part Two

Delivering the Speech

Chapter 7: Your Appearance and Demeanor When the Audience Isn't the Judge or Jury

Chapter 8: Using Your Body, Head, and Eyes

Chapter 9: Using Gestures

Chapter 10: Using Your Voice

Chapter 11: Eliminating Distracting Habits

Chapter 12: Using Your Notes

Chapter 13: Using Visual Aids

Chapter 7

Your Appearance and Demeanor When the Audience Isn't the Judge or Jury

7.1 Appropriate Attire

You've been invited to speak at a luncheon meeting of the local Rotary Club. You know a few of the members and have been their guest at previous luncheon meetings. Some members attend these meetings wearing casual clothing. Others dress more formally in business attire. As the invited speaker how should you dress?

Always recognize that when invited to speak, you are appearing in your role as a lawyer, and your audience expects to see one. Dress that way. Regardless of how well you know members of the audience and how you think they will be dressed, you should dress as the professional invited to speak. Not only does this satisfy the audience members' expectations, it expresses the respect that you have for them and for yourself.

Dress as you would if you were appearing in court or meeting with a client. Figures 7.1-a, 7.1-b, and 7.1-c display the typical attire that would be appropriate. Strive for a conservative look. Your suit should be black, gray, navy or brown. It is acceptable for a woman to wear either a skirted suit or a pantsuit. Men should wear a well-pressed, plain shirt. White is the best choice. A woman's blouse can have a conservative pattern (Figure 7.1-c). Men must avoid loud ties. In Figure 7.1-d, the speaker is dressed professionally, but his shirt is too dark and his tie too busy.

If there is no doubt that the event does not call for courtroom attire, choose business casual attire. It's common to see male speakers—most often politicians—appear in a suit but no tie, hoping to convey a relaxed-formal air. Instead, this presents a sloppy, careless appearance (Figure 7.1-e). A sport shirt and jacket are a better choice.

Men should wear polished dress shoes (black or brown) and dark socks. Women should wear conservatively-colored dress shoes or closed-toe heels.

Your hair must be neatly groomed in a conservative style. Men's facial hair should be well-groomed and neat (Figures 7.1-b and 7.1-d). Of course, your hair, face, and hands should be clean. Cologne and perfume are acceptable if lightly applied.

7.2 Appropriate Attitude and Behavior

Behave professionally. Even if some audience members are your friends, take the situation seriously. Don't be dour, however. Your audience should regard you as friendly and approachable.

Adopt a conversational tone and speak enthusiastically, but don't overplay it. Your audience will be able to detect insincerity, so act naturally and don't exaggerate your cheerfulness.

Do not condescend, especially when speaking to lay audiences. The fact that you are a lawyer does not make you superior to the audience. Fight the impulse to become impatient when members of a lay audience have difficulty understanding your topic. Remember, these audience members have no legal training and, likely, are struggling to grasp what to you are simple concepts.

Be especially careful to be genuine when addressing young audiences. Don't talk down to them, but don't pretend to be one of them. They best way to relate to young audiences during a speech is to behave like an adult.

Figures 7.1-a Proper Attire

Figure 7.1-b Proper Attire

Figure 7.1-c Proper Attire

Figure 7.1-d Dark Shirt and Loud Tie

Figure 7.1-e Relaxed-Formal Look

Sources

Detz, Joan, *It's Not What You Say, It's How You Say It.* New York: St. Martin's Griffin, 2000.

Farmer, Ann. "Order in the Closet: Why Attire for Women Lawyers is Still an Issue." Retrieved from https://www.americanbar.org/content/dam/aba/publishing/perspectives_magazine/2010_fall.authcheckdam.pdf.

Kane, Sally. "Law Office Dress Code for Men and Women." Retrieved from https://www.thebalance.com/sample-law-firm-dress-code-2164257.

Chapter 8

Using Your Body, Head, and Eyes

8.1 Posture and Presence

A. Three-Step Technique for Perfect Posture

Strong posture conveys confidence, credibility, and control. An easy three-step technique for maintaining good posture is illustrated in Figures 8.1-a,

Figure 8.1-a Perfect Posture Step One

Figure 8.1-b Perfect Posture Step Two

Figure 8.1-c Perfect Posture Step Three

8.1-b, and 8.2-c. First, with your arms at your sides, bend your elbows to raise your forearms facing forward and parallel to the ground. Your palms should face each other (Figure 8.1-a). Next, keeping your elbows at your sides, pivot your arms at the elbows out to the side, perpendicular to your body (Figure 8.1-b). Finally, twist your wrists so that your palms face up (Figure 8.1-c). The result—perfect posture (Figure 8.1-d). Practice this technique every time you stand and, eventually, strong posture will become second nature to you.

Figure 8.1-d Perfect Posture

B. Convey a Strong Presence

Take command of the stage to convey a strong presence to the audience. It's most effective to speak without a lectern, because speaking without a lectern conveys confidence and helps you build a rapport with the audience. It also provides you with the ability to move about the stage (Figure 8.1-e).

If you must use a lectern, stand a short distance behind it (Figure 8.1-f) and do not lean or lay your arms and hands on it (Figures 8.1-g and 8.1-h).

Figure 8.1-e Stand Next to the Lectern

Figure 8.1-f Standing Behind the Lectern

Figure 8.1-g Hands on the Lectern

Figure 8.1-h Leaning on the Lectern

8.2 Using Purposeful Movements

Effective movement on stage adds variety and meaning to your speech. These movements, however, must have a purpose. If the movement does not reinforce your words, stand still. Pacing and wandering while speaking— movement for movement's sake—is distracting and annoying to your audience. Plan and practice your movements so that they appear natural and are appropriate to the thought you're conveying.

A. Transitional Movement Between Points

Movements work well to signal transitions from point to point. The "diamond" pattern is most commonly used for this purpose. During the opening, stand near the center of the room. Move toward the right when transitioning to the first point, move to the center for the second point, and move to the left for the third. Move to your starting point for the speech's conclusion (Figure 8.2-a). Move immediately before each point and stay in position while speaking about the point.

Figure 8.2-a Diamond Pattern

B. Movement for Emphasis and Dramatic Effect

From center stage step closer to the audience to emphasize a point or to add dramatic effect (Figure 8.2-b).

Figure 8.2-b Move Close for Emphasis

C. Moving Away from the Audience

Walk on a diagonal when moving away from the audience (Figure 8.2-c). Only turn your back to the audience during a transition from one point to another when you are not speaking.

Figure 8.2-c Moving Away From the Audience

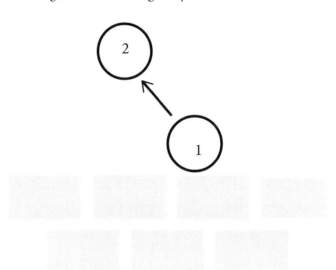

D. Point of View Movement (Pro and Con)

When using the Compare/Contrast speech, move from one position on stage to another when you transition from one point of view regarding the topic to another. Unless you want to emphasize one point of view as superior to the other (move closer to the audience), the movement should take you to a position on the same plane as the first (Figure 8.2-d).

Figure 8.2-d Changing Point of View Pattern

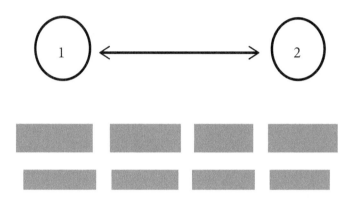

8.3 Maintaining Eye Contact with the Audience

A successful speaker builds a rapport with each audience member. Maintaining eye contact with audience members is the strongest method of building a rapport with them. The audience members will feel as though you are speaking to them individually.

While speaking, look at an audience member in the eyes for at least the time it takes you to complete a sentence or thought. Turning your head and body (not just your eyes), scan the room and randomly stop to focus on a listener. In Figure 8.3-a, the speaker's eye contact is ineffective because she moves

Figure 8.3-a Weak Eye Contact—No Head or Body Movement

Figure 8.3-b Strong Eye Contact

only her eyes. The speaker in Figure 8.3-b, however, maintains excellent eye contact with the entire audience by moving her head and body, not just her eyes. Vary your gaze's location—front section, back section, middle section, right section, left section—so that you have eye contact with as many individuals as possible.

When speaking to a large audience you may encounter a problem maintaining eye contact if the venue uses stage lighting. Although the lighting makes it easy for the audience to see you, it will "blind" you so that you can see, at most, only the first few rows. Don't let this "spotlight blindness" rattle you. Don't squint. Don't look only at the rows that you can see. Instead, just as you would in a smaller space, scan and gaze—front, back, middle, right, left—so that it appears as though you can see the entire audience and that you are focusing on individual audience members.

Sources

Dempsey, David J. *Legally Speaking: 40 Powerful Presentation Principles Lawyers Need to Know.* New York: Kaplan Publishing, 2009.

O'Hair, Dan, Hannah Rubenstein, and Rob Stewart. *A Pocket Guide to Public Speaking.* New York: Bedford/St. Martin's, 2016.

Chapter 9

Using Gestures

9.1 Purposeful Gesturing

Gestures are a speech's seasoning. Just as too much, too little, or unsuitable seasoning can ruin a recipe, using too many, too few, or inappropriate gestures can ruin a speech. On the other hand, sprinkling in just the right amount of appropriate gestures will make your speech marvelous.

Use gestures sparingly and with a purpose. They should reinforce your points and maintain the audience's attention. Unplanned, impulsive arm and hand movements—"talking with your hands"—serve no purpose and distract the audience. In other words, gestures should call attention to your ideas and not to themselves.

To ensure that your gestures serve their purpose, don't leave them up to chance. Plan and practice how and when to use your arms and hands and when to keep them still.

The most effective gestures should appear to be spontaneous. Therefore, craft your speech and then, while practicing, note what gestures come naturally and where they arise. Decide whether the ideas expressed at these points require the gestures as support and whether the gestures accomplish this purpose. If there is no purpose, there should be no gesture. On the other hand, if a gesture is helpful, work to perfect it.

9.2 Gestures—What to Use and What to Avoid

A. Gestures to Use

The following gestures are effective when used purposefully:

1. Counting

Use your fingers to count items as you list them (Figure 9.2-a). Always start with your index finger and not your thumb. Using your thumb is awkward and looks as though you are aiming a gun at the audience (Figure 9.2-b).

Figure 9.2-a Counting Gesture

Figure 9.2-b Thumb-Gun Counting

2. Increase/Decrease—Small/Medium/Large (Figure 9.2-c)

3. On the Other Hand/This or That (Figure 9.2-d)

4. A Tiny Bit (Figure 9.2-e)

5. Pointing with an Open Hand

This gesture is used most often during the question and answer session to recognize an audience member (Figure 9.2-f). Use it in place of pointing your index finger (Figure 9.2-g). Pointing with the index finger is often interpreted by audience members as hostile and intimidating.

Figure 9.2-f Open Hand Point

Figure 9.2-g Aggressive Point

B. Gestures to Avoid

In addition to any gestures that do not serve a purpose, avoid using distracting gestures that draw the audience members' attention away from the speech.

1. Air Quotation Marks

People use this gesture to convey suspicion about or distain for an idea they are expressing. It conveys a discourteous manner (Figure 9.2-h).

Figure 9.2-h Air Quotation Marks

2. "Politician Thumb-Point"

This gesture has been adopted as a substitute for pointing the index finger. Although it eliminates the hostility of pointing, it is overused by politicians and has become a cliché (Figure 9.2-i).

Figure 9.2-i Politician Thumb-Point

3. Pounding on the Lectern
4. Spread Fingers — "Jazz Hands" (Figure 9.2-j)

Figure 9.2-j Jazz Hands

5. Over-Broad Gestures—Outside the Gesture Zone

Keep your gestures within the "gesture zone." The zone forms a rectangle from just below your shoulders to your waist and extends about two feet beyond each side of your body (Figures 9.2-k and 9.2-k2).

Figure 9.2-k Gesture Zone

Figure 9.2-k2 Gestures Outside the Zone

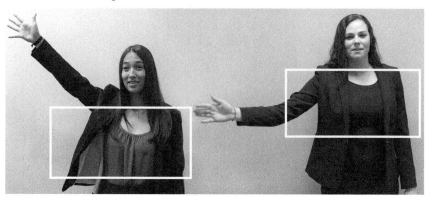

When standing behind a lectern, however, adjust the zone so that your gestures are not hidden (Figure 9.2-l).

Figure 9.2-l Gesture Zone at Lectern

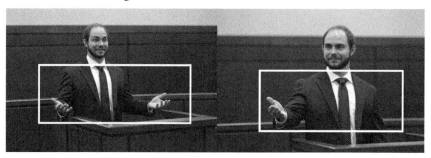

6. Choppy and Repetitive Movements

Vary your gestures and make them smoothly. If you use a gesture repeatedly, audience members will focus on your movements instead of your content.

7. Cramped Counting (Figure 9.2-m)

Keep your hand in the gesture zone when counting.

Figure 9.2-m Cramped Counting

8. Holding an Object While Gesturing (Figure 9.2-n)

Never bring a pen to the lectern. It will serve no purpose during the speech except to distract from what you are saying.

Figure 9.2-n Gesturing with Object

9.3 The Ready Position—What to Do When Not Gesturing

Your arms and hands should move only when the movement is necessary. Otherwise, keep them motionless in the "Ready Position." This position will minimize the tendency to "talk with your hands" and the distracting habit of touching your face and hair (Figure 9.3-a). An effective ready position will help you move smoothly into and out of gestures.

Figure 9.3-a Hands on Face and Hair

A. Effective Ready Positions

There are several ready positions that you can use. Choose one that comes naturally and is appropriate for the topic, venue, and audience. Practice using each technique to see which works best.

1. Arms at Your Sides (Figure 9.3-b)

Figure 9.3-b Ready Position Arms at Sides

2. One Bent Elbow

One arm bent at your elbow and the dominant arm at your side (Figure 9.3-c). If you are using note cards, hold the cards with the hand on the bent arm and gesture with the other (Figure 9.3-d).

Figure 9.3-c Ready Position One Arm Bent

Figure 9.3-d Ready Position Holding Notes

3. Hands Together, in Front, at Belt Level

- One hand wrapped over the other (Figure 9.3-e).

Figure 9.3-e One Hand Wrapped Over the Other

- Steeple your fingertips (Figure 9.3-f).

Figure 9.3-f Steepled Fingers

B. Ready Positions to Avoid

1. Interlocking Fingers

In addition to looking awkward, this makes it difficult to smoothly move into a gesture (Figure 9.3-g).

Figure 9.3-g Interlocking Fingers

2. The Fig Leaf (Figure 9.3-h)

In addition to looking awkward, this position makes moving into gestures difficult.

Figure 9.3-h The Fig Leaf

3. Crossed Arms (Figure 9.3-i)

This confrontational position conveys a challenging attitude. It is a difficult position for moving into gestures.

Figure 9.3-i Crossed Arms

4. Hands on Hips (Figure 9.3-j)

Like crossed arms, this position is unwelcoming, and conveys aggression. It too makes it difficult to move into gestures.

Figure 9.3-j Hands on Hips

5. Hands behind Your Back (Figure 9.3-k)

Think of this as a "reversed" fig leaf.

Figure 9.3-k Hands Behind Back

6. Hands in your pockets (Figure 9.3-l)

This position is sloppy and too casual. Pockets will handcuff you, preventing fluid gesturing.

Figure 9.3-l   Hands in Pockets

7. The Model Pose (Figure 9.3-m)

Although this pose may look "cool" in photographs, it displays smug over-confidence.

Figure 9.3-m The Model Pose

Sources

Dempsey, David J. *Legally Speaking: 40 Powerful Presentation Principles Lawyers Need to Know.* New York: Kaplan Publishing, 2009.

O'Hair, Dan, Hannah Rubenstein, and Rob Stewart. *A Pocket Guide to Public Speaking.* New York: Bedford/St. Martin's, 2016.

Van Edwards, Vanessa. "20 Hand Gestures You Should Be Using." Retrieved from http://www.huffingtonpost.com/vanessa-van-edwards/20-hand-gestures-you-shou_b_8034618.html.

Chapter 10

Using Your Voice

When you speak, you use a variety of tools—gestures, movement, eye contact, and visual aids. The most important tool at your disposal, however, is your voice. Your voice communicates your ideas and creates the audience's impression of you and the speech.

10.1 Vocal Variety

Adopt a conversational tone when speaking and vary volume, pitch, pace, and pauses to keep your audience engaged. Increase and decrease volume and pitch, slow your rate of speaking and include pauses to emphasize important points, to add dramatic effect and to avoid a sleep-inducing monotone.

10.2 Vary Purposefully

As with gesturing and moving, varying your vocal quality must be purposeful and controlled. Plan and practice your vocal techniques so that they enhance rather than hinder your message.

1. Volume and Projection

Keep your voice audible when decreasing your volume for effect. The emphasis or dramatic effect will be lost if the audience can't hear you. When raising your volume, take care not to yell at the audience.

2. Vocal Quality—Pitch

Control how and when you raise and lower your pitch. Uncontrolled pitch changes can result in the annoying "sing-song" pattern we often use when speaking with children. Also, avoid pitch changes resulting in "up-talking"— the irritating habit of ending sentences with an upward-moving pitch as though you are asking a question (Chapter 11).

3. Pace

Control the changes in your rate of speaking. Speaking too slowly will bore, not engage. Speaking too quickly will limit the audience members' ability to understand and retain what you say.

4. Pauses

Use pauses for variety, clarity, and dramatic effect. For example:

- Pause between items in a list.

  "There are several requirements for a deed to be valid: [pause] legal capacity, [pause] a vested interest, [pause] nominal considerations [pause]...."

- Pause to create anticipation and suspense.

  "The jury foreman stood to read the verdict. [pause] 'Guilty.'"

- Pause before a quotation.

  "Justice Lewis Powell once said, [pause] 'I am primarily a lawyer. I would rather play in the game than be the umpire.'"

- Pause while the audience laughs.

Be mindful of the length of your pauses. Dramatic and emphatic pauses should be long enough to build anticipation or to emphasize a point, but not so long as to frustrate the audience. That said, pause longer than you think is appropriate. Your perception of time becomes distorted when you give a speech.

"Punctuate" with brief pauses between sentences and paragraphs. Otherwise, the audience will become exhausted listening to you "machine-gun" through the speech. Consider the impact of Franklin Delano Roosevelt's first inaugural address in 1933 had he not used punctuation pauses.

This great Nation will endure as it has endured will revive and will prosper so first of all let me assert my firm belief that the only thing we

*have to fear is fear itself nameless unreasoning unjustified terror which
paralyzes needed efforts to convert retreat into advance in every dark
hour of our national life a leadership of frankness and vigor has met with
that understanding and support of the people themselves which is essential
to victory I am convinced that you will again give that support to leadership in these critical days.*

Whew!

10.3 Vocal Warmups

Your larynx, tongue, lips and diaphragm are muscles that require warmups
to improve performance and to prevent injury.

A. Articulation Exercises

Repeating tongue twisters is an excellent warmup technique that strengthens
and loosens your lips and tongue to improve the quality of your articulation
and diction.

The following are examples of tongue twisters that should become part of
a daily regimen to perfect articulation and diction. Repeat the phrase going
faster and faster each time. Focus on pronouncing each consonant crisply and
each vowel clearly.

Unique New York, New York Unique

Peggy Babcock

Leave the lazy lion alone

Six thick thistle sticks

Mixed biscuits

Red leather yellow leather red lorry yellow lorry

Wild winds and wet weather

Frothy coffee

Rubber baby buggy bumpers

Any noise annoys an oyster but a noisy noise annoys an oyster most

A tutor who tooted the flute tried to tutor two young tooters to toot. Said
the two to the tutor, "Is it harder to toot or to tutor two tooters to toot?"

B. Breathing Exercises

Vocal power and volume require proper breathing with a strong diaphragm. This exercise will help you "oxygenate" and strengthen your breathing. Repeat the steps several times.

1. Stand erect, keeping your shoulders relaxed.

2. Relax your stomach.

3. Place your hands on your stomach and slowly inhale through your nose while counting to five. You should feel your stomach rise as your diaphragm contracts and moves downward.

4. Hold your breath for a count of five.

5. Exhale through your mouth to the count of five. Your stomach should tighten as your diaphragm relaxes and moves upward.

Sources

Dempsey, David J. *Legally Speaking: 40 Powerful Presentation Principles Lawyers Need to Know.* New York: Kaplan Publishing, 2009.

Detz, Joan. *It's Not What You Say, It's How You Say It.* New York: St. Martin's Griffin, 2000.

Marshall, Lisa B. "Vocal Exercises for Better Public Speaking." ßRetrieved from https://www.quickanddirtytips.com/business-career/public-speaking/vocal-exercises-for-better-public-speaking.

"Vocal Warm Ups for Public Speakers." Retrieved from https://www.write-out-loud.com/vocal-warm-ups.html#voicewarmups.

Chapter 11

Eliminating Distracting Habits

Audience members do not keep a list of your distracting habits or tally how many times they appear in a speech. They notice them, however, and are distracted by them.

It's very easy to spot the distracting habits of others and very easy to tell others to stop doing these things. Noticing our own habits, recognizing our faults, is difficult. We are rarely aware that we have them.

The following tips should help you identify and eliminate these habits.

A. Vocal Fillers

Um, like, so, ah, er, now, you know, clearly

There are very few of us who don't have the habit of saying these words while speaking. They clutter the speech, give the impression that you are not confident, and distract the audience. These fillers are a subconscious way of filling in space between sentences. You need to convert them into conscious occurrences and then concentrate on eliminating them.

This habit is difficult to break, because usually, we are not aware that we have it. The first step is to make yourself mindful of how and when you use vocal fillers by reviewing recordings of your practice sessions and by having friends point them out during conversations. Once you have diagnosed the problem, use practice sessions and conversations to stop the fillers from appearing between sentences. Speak more slowly than usual and make a conscious effort to pause and allow for a bit of silence between sentences. At first you will need to deliberately fight the urge to utter a filler. After repeated practice, however, it will become second nature for you to replace the vocal fillers with silence.

Now, So

There's a particular issue with "now" and "so." These two words are often used as transitions at the beginning of sentences. Although they may occasionally serve as acceptable transition words, it is easy to fall into the habit of unconsciously over-using them. Therefore, eliminate these transitions to avoid habitually using them as vocal fillers.

you guys

Although technically not a vocal filler, it is a vocal habit that should be eliminated. Referring to the audience as "you guys" is seldom appropriate. First, it is too informal for most of your speaking occasions. Second, "gals" as well as "guys" will be in the audience, so you will offend the women when you say it.

The only time that "you guys" might be appropriate is when you are speaking to an audience of close friends. Even then, don't use it. The only way to break the habit is to stop it completely.

B. "Up-Talking"

"Up-talking" is the habit of ending a declarative sentence with an upward-moving pitch, as though you are asking a question. It is often referred to as "Valley Girl" speech—this habit, however, is not limited to women. Eliminating this habit should be of particular concern to lawyers, because up-talking speakers sound insecure, lacking confidence in what they are saying. Unfortunately, as with vocal fillers, it is difficult to recognize that you have this annoying habit. Therefore, review practice-session recordings and rely on colleagues to detect it.

One method of eliminating up-talking is to have friends and colleagues point out when you fall into this habit. Another method, less annoying to your friends and colleagues, requires the simple exercise of reading aloud. As you read, make a conscious effort to drop your tone of voice at the end of every sentence. Perform this exercise often and record yourself so that you can objectively evaluate your progress.

C. Distracting Gestures

Uncontrolled gestures, "talking with your hands," serve no purpose other than to distract and annoy the audience. These gestures and other unconscious mannerisms such as touching your face, playing with your hair, and picking at fingernails should be identified and eliminated.

Review recordings of your practice sessions to identify your use of distracting gestures. Follow the steps outlined in Chapter 9 for controlling them and for using purposeful gestures.

D. Distracting Movements

1. Swaying and Rocking

To eliminate swaying and rocking while speaking, stand with your feet shoulder width apart. Point your toes forward, keeping your feet parallel. Slightly bend your knees and place your weight on the balls of your feet. Do not lean forward, however, or you will lose your balance.

2. Pacing

Pacing around the stage is generated by converting nervous energy into movement. Don't attempt to keep yourself from moving. Instead, transform the pacing into planned and practiced purposeful movements as described in Chapter 8.

> **A word of caution**: You have developed your distracting habits throughout your lifetime. It is very likely, therefore, that despite performing the exercises, you will occasionally fall back into these habits during a speech. Don't let this rattle you. No one is perfect.

Sources

Dempsey, David J. *Legally Speaking: 40 Powerful Presentation Principles Lawyers Need to Know*. New York: Kaplan Publishing, 2009.

O'Hair, Dan, Hannah Rubenstein, and Rob Stewart. *A Pocket Guide to Public Speaking*. New York: Bedford/St. Martin's, 2016.

Chapter 12

Using Your Notes

12.1 The Importance of Using Notes (Don't Memorize)

Lawyers learn to commit a great deal of information to memory. You may be tempted to use this skill when speaking publicly, because it will demonstrate your "command" of the information and, perhaps, because it will impress your audience. Even lawyers, however, are human. Humans forget things and lose track of their thoughts. All the best speakers, being human, use some system of notes to keep themselves on track.

Memorizing a presentation is simply not an option for the vast majority of speakers. For most people, it's a sure recipe for disaster. For one thing, it's just about impossible to remember everything, which all but guarantees that you'll come up blank at some point. The type of speeches that you'll present in your role as a lawyer will usually contain a great deal of information that can't be memorized easily. Informative and persuasive speeches require references to data, statistics, statutes, cases names, case citations, and quotations. Using notes is the only way to ensure that you present the information accurately.

Using notes also ensures that your delivery will be effective. Your goal is to be conversational while speaking. Memorized recitations are stilted and mechanical.

12.2 Types of Notes and How to Create Them

A. Simple Steps for Preparing Notes

There are several note systems that a speaker can use—sheets of paper, note cards, slideware, and electronic devices. Regardless of the system that you use, always use the following three steps to craft your notes.

1. First, outline your speech.

2. Then underline key words in the outline.

3. Use these key words, quotations, statistics and sources to form the content of your notes, creating an "outline" of your outline.

B. Sheet(s) of Paper

This technique can be useful when you speak at a lectern. Otherwise, using sheets of paper can be distracting and unmanageable.

1. Use bullet points and words rather than full sentences (Figure 12.2-a). You must be able to quickly glance at your notes. You won't be able to read full sentences while speaking. Keep the notes to as few pages as possible—one page is best. Do not use your outline as notes.

Figure 12.2-a Simple Page of Notes

2. If using several pages, do not staple or otherwise bind them. You must be able to slip pages behind the others as you use them. As Figure 12.2-b illustrates, flipping pages is awkward and distracting.

Figure 12.2-b Awkward Flipping of Pages

3. Keep the paper on the lectern. Avoid holding the paper in your hands, especially if you are moving about the stage (Figure 12.2-c).

Figure 12.2-c Avoid Holding Notes with Two Hands

4. There are two significant disadvantages when using sheets of paper as a note system.

   • Using sheets of paper limits your movement around the stage, because you must remain close enough to the lectern to read the notes. As Figure 12.2-d shows, it is awkward and distracting if you must walk to the lectern or turn to view your notes on the lectern.

Figure 12.2-d Glancing at Notes on Lectern

   • You are likely to include too much detail on sheets of paper. Figure 12.2-e shows a page of "notes" that would work well as an outline but contains too much text to be useful while speaking.

Figure 12.2-e Too Much Detail

C. Note Cards (Figure 12.2-f)

Figure 12.2-f Note Card

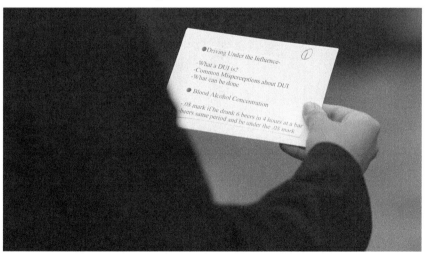

Note cards are versatile and afford you the flexibility to move about the stage without being anchored to the lectern. They are convenient to hold and permit free use of gestures.

1. Use large size index cards. 4x6 are preferable to 3x5.

2. Write on only one side of the card.

3. Place a limited amount of information on each card. Use bullet points and simple words rather than full sentences.

4. If typed, use a large font. If printed, use large, legible letters.

5. Number the cards in case you drop them or they get out of order.

6. The best way to hold note cards is illustrated in Figure 12.2-g. The speaker holds the cards in her non-dominant hand leaving the other arm and hand free to gesture. Bending the elbow positions the cards so that the speaker can easily glance down at them. Don't move the cards from hand to hand or grab them with both hands (Figure 12.2-h). Never gesture with the hand holding the cards (Figure 12.2-i).

7. When you finish using a notecard, slide it behind the remaining cards.

Figure 12.2-g Best Way to Hold Note Cards

Figure 12.2-h Two-Handed Grab

Figure 12.2-i Gesturing with Note Cards

D. Slideware Programs and Electronic Devices

Speakers often use slides projected by slideware programs for the dual pur-pose of serving as visual aids and as a note system. Although this method is a favorite of many speakers and is often recommended, its weaknesses far out-weigh its benefits, if any.

1. Using this visual aid to serve as your notes forces you to repeatedly turn your head and body away from the audience to look at the screen while you are speaking.

2. Using slides as your notes significantly diminishes their value as visual aids. You will use too many slides, some of which would not be helpful as visual aids, because you'll need a slide for every point you make. You'll include too much information on the slides, much

of which might be appropriate for note purposes but not helpful to your audience.

3. You run the risk of losing your notes if you encounter technical difficulties with the slideware program during the speech.

In addition to slideware programs, rapid advances in technology have resulted in the availability of many other electronic note systems offering software that can be used on tablets, smartphones, notebooks and other portable electronic devices. Although cutting edge, they are not without disadvantages. Manipulation and placement of the devices during a speech can be awkward. Moreover, as with slideware programs, you will be at the mercy of the technology's reliability. If the device or software malfunctions, you will not have the benefit of notes.

12.3 Using Notes Correctly— The PG-EC-RS Technique

[Pause and Glance-Regain Eye Contact-Resume Speaking]

A common self-criticism by speakers is that, "I relied on my notes too much." There is nothing wrong, however, in relying on notes during a speech. Notes are there to be used, and audience members expect you to use them.

Typically, when the speaker seems to be relying on notes "too much," the actual problem is that the speaker is not using the notes properly. The speaker keeps talking while consulting the notes, reading to the audience from the notes. The speaker loses eye contact with the audience, and, consequently, loses the connection with the audience.

Using notes correctly involves a few simple steps that I call the PG-EC-RS Technique.

1. Pause speaking, then

2. *Briefly* Glance at the notes.

3. Regain Eye Contact with the audience, and then

4. Resume Speaking.

The pause and brief glance are vital for effectively using notes. Pausing gives you time to digest the note. It also gives audience members a moment to process what you've said. Most importantly, it prevents you from reading to the audience. The key is to stop speaking long enough to view the notes. Recognize that the length of the pause will seem longer to you than it does to your audience. Don't start speaking again until you have regained eye contact with the audience. It's important to practice this technique so that the steps flow smoothly.

Practice your speech often enough to internalize your presentation, focusing on the ideas behind the words. As part of your preparation, become completely familiar with every part of it. Practice aloud, until you are comfortable delivering the speech without the use of notes. Rehearse as many times as you need to. That will reduce your need for notes in the first place.

Notes are not to be used, however, as a way to read the speech. They serve the purpose of keeping you on track, reminding you of what you'll be saying.

Sources

Dempsey, David J. *Legally Speaking: 40 Powerful Presentation Principles Lawyers Need to Know*. New York: Kaplan Publishing, 2009.

O'Hair, Dan, Hannah Rubenstein, and Rob Stewart. *A Pocket Guide to Public Speaking*. New York: Bedford/St. Martin's, 2016.

Carillo, Frank. "Using Notes in Presentations. Is it okay?" *The Total Communicator*. Retrieved at http://totalcommunicator.com/vol3_5/expert5.html.

Chapter 13

Using Visual Aids

13.1 Purpose of Visual Aids

Well-crafted visual aids can be invaluable to a speech's effectiveness when used properly. People remember more information when audio and visual matter convey the information.

On the other hand, if the visual aids are not well-crafted, not professional, and are not used effectively, the speech can be a failure. Rather than grab the audience's interest, the visual aids distract audience members from your message.

Always keep in mind that a visual aid must do just that—aid the speech. Using visual aids merely because you can is a mistake.

13.2 Deciding Whether to Use Visual Aids

Too often, speakers choose a visual aid style and select visual aid content before writing the speech. The speech, therefore, becomes subservient to the visual aid. Your first consideration should be the speech, its ideas and points. Not every speech needs visual aids, and not every idea in a speech requires them either. Write the speech first, practice it at least once, and then consider whether the audience's understanding will be helped by supplementing the presentation with a visual aid. Then consider what type of aid will best serve the purpose and determine what information should be supplied in the visual aid.

Audience analysis (Chapter 2) will help you to determine whether you need to use visual aids.

Consider the following questions:

- What level of knowledge do audience members have about the topic? Is your audience the type that will require visual aids to understand the concepts that you are discussing?

- Is your audience the type that will lose interest without visual aid stimulation?

- Will visual aids distract audience members from the speech's substance?

- Do the visual aids become the focus of the speech? Is the speech about the visual aids or are the visual aids about the speech?

- When practicing your speech using the visual aids, do you find yourself spending more time explaining visual aids than explaining your points?

- Are there too many visual aids?

- Will visual aids clutter the ideas by competing for attention with your points?

- Will you exhaust and distract your audience by displaying too many visual aids?

13.3 Types of Visual Aids and Techniques for Using Them

"Visual aid" is not a synonym for "projected slides." Technology has made it too easy for us to believe that slideware must be used when speaking. There are a variety of visual aids that can and should be used. Take a step back and evaluate which of these would be best for your presentation.

A. Objects and Props

Objects and props are useful, because they physically represent ideas. For example, you are speaking to an audience of elementary school children about how laws are enacted. After practicing your speech and analyzing your audience, you decide that children would be more engaged in the speech if you used a visual aid. Because elementary school children would relate to a physical object representing what otherwise is an abstract idea, you decide that a tangible example of "laws" would be useful. Therefore, you choose a statute book as a visual aid (Figures 13.3-a and 13.3-b).

Figure 13.3-a Object as Visual Aid

The object must be large enough to be seen by the entire audience. For example, the apple in Figure 13.3-c would be effective for a small audience in a small room. It would not be effective, however, in a large room with a large audience.

Figure 13.3-b Object as Visual Aid

Figure 13.3-c Context Determines If Size Is Right

You must have a convenient way to display the object and to keep it hidden from view. Display the object only when it is relevant to your point. Otherwise, hide it from view to avoid distracting the audience.

B. Handouts

Handouts are helpful if the topic is complex and will be difficult for the audience to digest. They also allow you to provide detail that you may not have the time to cover in the speech. Handouts are especially useful to a lay audience learning about legal concepts and to lawyers attending continuing legal education sessions. A handout also serves as an excellent marketing tool by placing your firm's letterhead on the handout.

During the speech, inform the audience that handouts will be available, and distribute them after you present the speech. Handouts provided before or during the speech will compete with you for the audience's attention.

C. Photographs

Photographs must be large enough to be seen by every audience member. Have a convenient method of displaying them. Practice using the photographs so that you smoothly display and remove them from view.

D. Flip Charts and White Boards

The only justification for using flip charts and white boards is to compile information that audience members contribute during the speech. Otherwise, always use visual aids prepared in advance.

Flip charts and white boards have several disadvantages. Unless you are a contortionist, you will have to turn your back when writing, making it difficult for audience members to hear you speak. The only solution is to stop talking when writing—a "solution" that disrupts the speech's rhythm. Also, without a great deal of practice, it is difficult to write neatly and legibly. Finally, flipping the chart pages is awkward and erasing material from white boards is messy.

E. Video and Audio

Video and audio clips are excellent attention-grabbing methods. They should be short—usually no longer than a minute or two.

The primary concern about using video and audio clips is the danger that they may malfunction and that they will be awkward to play. Practice using them and have them cued up and ready to go.

F. Document Camera and Overhead Transparencies

Document cameras and overheads are useful for displaying and annotating documents without needing to hand them out to the audience.

G. Slideware Presentation Programs

Slideware presentation programs such as PowerPoint and Prezi are the ubiquitous visual aid method used by speakers. When used correctly they serve speakers and their speeches well. When used poorly, however, they sabotage the presentation and torture the audience. Reflect on the times when you've been forced to sit through presentations that painfully misuse slideware. The speaker displays slides containing paragraph after paragraph of text and reads them to you or flashes them so quickly that you haven't enough time to read them. Every point that the speaker makes is accompanied by a slide so that the "speech" becomes a narrated slide show. You spend more time looking at the screen than looking at and listening to the speaker.

Ensure success by carefully composing and skillfully presenting the slides.

13.4 Designing and Using Slideware Presentation Programs

A. Slide Design — Composition and Layout

The only purpose that slides should serve is to quickly convey information supporting the point that you are making in the speech. Design slides so that they can be read easily, will support your message, and maintain your audience's interest. Slides that distract from you and your speech and draw attention to themselves are not visual "aids."

Principles of composition and layout are complex and could be covered in a text of their own. You do not need extensive training, however, or to be an expert in these principles to design effective slideware presentations. Attention to a few basic principles is sufficient.

1. Text

Font size must be large enough to be read by the entire audience. A safe choice is 30pt or larger.

Choose simple font styles and avoid the bizarre and fanciful. Experts recommend using sans serif fonts.

Limit the amount of text on each slide so that audience members can read the slides easily and quickly — strive for 3 seconds per slide. Use bullet points and short phrases rather than long sentences. Figure 13.4-a depicts a slide containing too much text. It would be impossible for audience members to read and digest this information. The slide in Figure 13.4-b, however, does a strong job of conveying information, because the amount of text is limited and audience members aren't required to read long, complicated sentences.

Figure 13.4-a Too Many Words

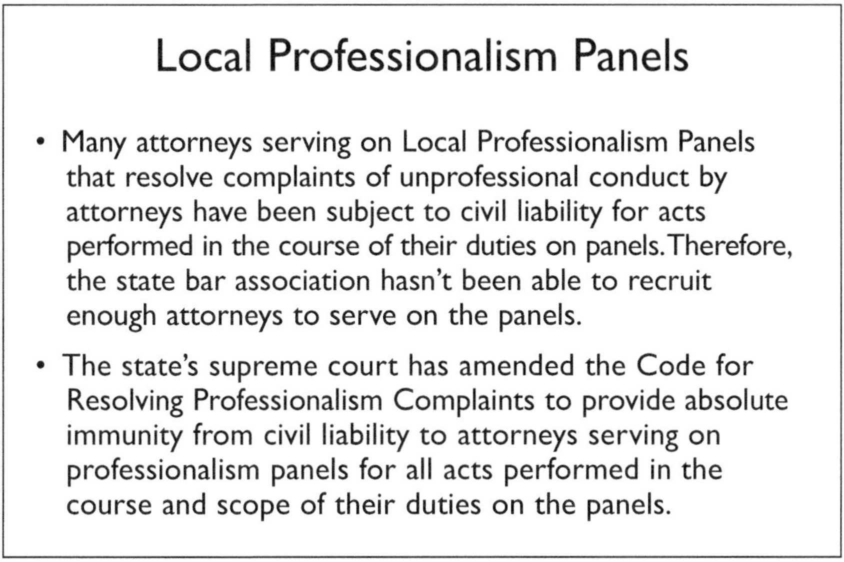

Local Professionalism Panels

- Many attorneys serving on Local Professionalism Panels that resolve complaints of unprofessional conduct by attorneys have been subject to civil liability for acts performed in the course of their duties on panels. Therefore, the state bar association hasn't been able to recruit enough attorneys to serve on the panels.

- The state's supreme court has amended the Code for Resolving Professionalism Complaints to provide absolute immunity from civil liability to attorneys serving on professionalism panels for all acts performed in the course and scope of their duties on the panels.

Figure 13.4-b Limited Amount of Text Conveys the Message

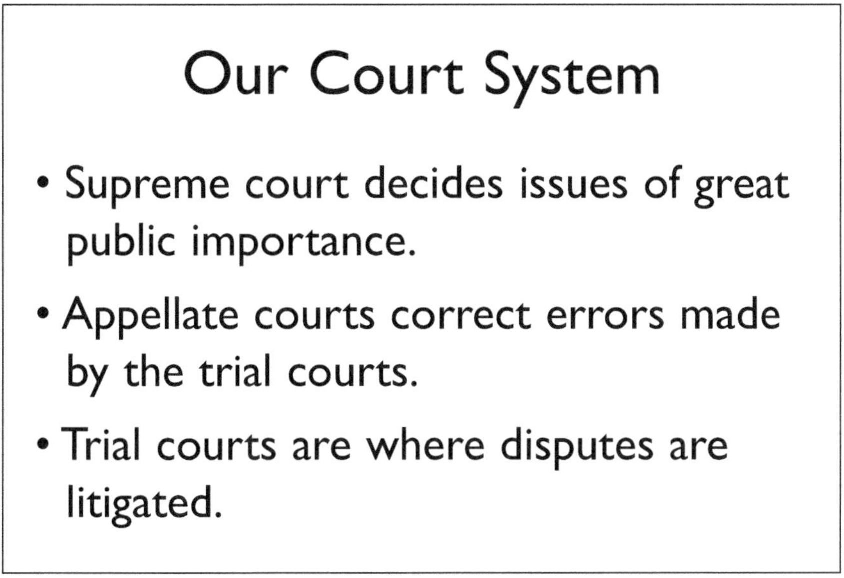

Our Court System

- Supreme court decides issues of great public importance.
- Appellate courts correct errors made by the trial courts.
- Trial courts are where disputes are litigated.

Figure 13.4-c is an excellent example of the kind of distracting and annoying slide that lawyers commonly inflict upon their audiences. In this example, the speaker is explaining the state's requirements for creating condominiums. Knowing that it is important for the audience to be aware of the relevant statute, the speaker projects a slide reproducing all of the provision's language. The slide, overloaded with text, is useless. The audience won't be able to and won't want to read it. If audience members do try to read it, they will not be listening to the speaker.

Figure 13.4-c Too Much Information

718.104 Creation of condominiums; contents of declaration. – Every condominium created in this state shall be created pursuant to this chapter.

(1) A condominium may be created on land owned in fee simple or held under a lease complying with the provisions of s. 718.401.

(2) A condominium is created by recording a declaration in the public records of the county where the land is located, executed and acknowledged with the requirements for a deed. All persons who have record title to the interest in the land being submitted to condominium ownership, or their lawfully authorized agents, must join in the execution of the declaration. Upon the recording of the declaration, or an amendment adding a phase to the condominium under s. 718.403(6), all units described in the declaration or phase amendment as being located in or on the land then being submitted to condominium ownership shall come into existence, regardless of the state of completion of planned improvements in which the units may be located or any other requirement or description that a declaration may provide. Upon recording the declaration of condominium pursuant to this section, the developer shall file the recording information with the division within 120 calendar days on a form prescribed by the division.

Figure 13.4-d on the other hand, depicts an ideal, reader-friendly slide for the situation. It uses bullet points rather than complete sentences and contains white space that draws attention to the words. It reinforces the speaker's message, because it encapsulates the key concepts that the speaker will address in detail about the statute. The statute's exact language should be provided to the audience in a handout after the presentation. In other words, if a copy of the slides you use in a speech can function as a handout, you've used too many slides containing too much information.

Figure 13.4-d Simplified and More Effective

Steps in Creating a Condominium

- Recording Declaration
- Filing Recording Information

2. Backgrounds, Colors, Bells and Whistles

Favor solid colors and simple backgrounds. There should be a strong contrast between the text and the background. It's best to place white text on a black background or black text on a white background.

Avoid the fancy animation and transition techniques provided by the programs. Many speakers use these features merely because they can rather than to serve a particular purpose. These features are counter-productive, because they draw attention to the bells and whistles and away from the speaker and the speaker's message.

3. Charts

In addition to displaying text and photographs, use slides to describe and compare data. As with text, avoid including too much detail that will be difficult to read and understand. Figure 13.4-e is far too cluttered and complex to work well as a visual aid. It contains too much text and too many "bars." Audience members wouldn't be able to digest and understand how the data compare without a lengthy explanation. On the other hand, the simple chart in Figure 13.4-f clearly demonstrates how the data compare.

Figure 13.4-e Complicated Chart

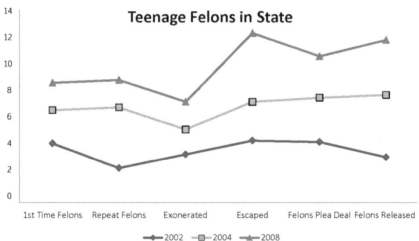

Figure 13.4-f Simple Accessible Chart

4. Rule of Thirds

Centering text and images makes for uninteresting slides. To create interest, compose slides following the Rule of Thirds. Use four imaginary lines to divide a slide into thirds—horizontally and vertically. Figure 13.4-g shows that the lines intersect in four places on the slide. To enhance the slide's impact and to create interest, compose the slide so that text and images are located along the lines and at those intersection points (Figure 13.4-h).

Figure 13.4-g Rule of Thirds

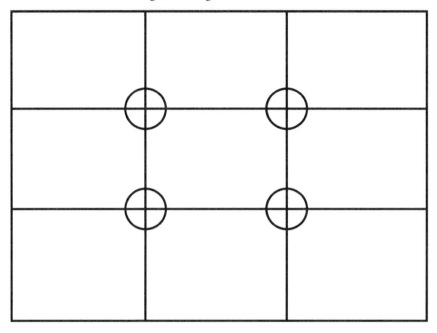

Figure 13.4-h Rule of Thirds in Action

Figure 13.4-i Weak Composition—Centered Text and Photograph

Figure 13.4-j Weak Composition—Centered Text

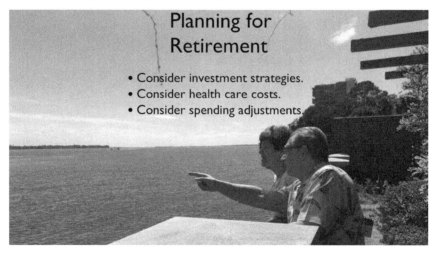

Figures 13.4-i and 13.4-j depict lackluster slides with centered texts and photographs. Figures 13.4-k and 13.4-l depict far more interesting slides because, in each, the text and photographs balance the composition.

Figure 13.4-k Improved Composition Using Rule of Thirds

Figure 13.4-l Improved Composition Using Rule of Thirds

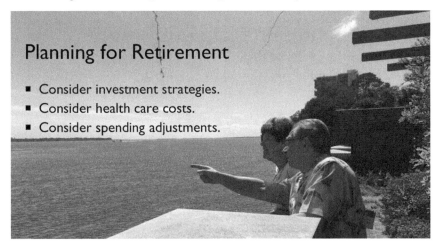

When applying the Rule of Thirds, strive to keep the slides uncluttered. Figure 13.4-m is too busy. Cluttered with photographs, it lacks dramatic impact. A stronger slide uses fewer photographs—choose the best of the group—and limited text to dramatically support the speaker's message (Figure 13.4-n).

Figure 13.4-m Cluttered Slide

Landscapes to be Protected

Figure 13.4-n Simple and Dramatic

Statute Protects Landscapes

Man Made Spaces

Decorative Spaces

5. Images of People

When including images of people, place them so that they are facing toward the slide's interior and content. In Figure 13.4-o, the police officer faces away from the slide's center and text. The viewer's eye is drawn away from the text. In Figure 13.4-p, the composition brings the photograph and text together. Figures 13.4-q and13.4-r also show the strength in composing the slide so that the people face center and the text.

Figure 13.4-o Weak Composition—Person Facing Away from Slide's Center

Figure 13.4-p Improved Compostion Person Facing into Slide

Figure 13.4-q Well-Composed Slide Person Facing Center

Figure 13.4-r Well-Composed Slide—Person Facing Center

B. Slide Presentation

Well-composed slides will be worthless if they are not presented properly. Following some simple delivery guidelines will ensure a successful presentation aided, not hampered, by slideware.

1. Practice using the slideware program with the equipment that you'll be using to project the slides.

2. Limit the number of slides that you use. Instead of projecting a slide for every point that you make, only use a slide when the point requires support. It's a speech, not a slide show.

3. Reveal the slide only when it is relevant to the point and remove it when it is no longer relevant. Use the "mute" function on the remote or build blank slides into the slide presentation.

4. When you project a slide containing text, give audience members time to read it before you speak. Audience members can't read the information and listen to you at the same time.

5. Do not read the entire slide to the audience.

6. Stand stage right (audience left) of the projection screen (Figure 13.4-s). Do not stand in front of the screen.

7. Use your left arm and hand to point to the slide (Figure 13.4-t). Otherwise you will be forced to turn your back on the audience (Figure 13.4-u). Keep your arm far enough from the screen to avoid blocking the projector light.

8. Talk to the audience, not the slide. Never turn your back to the audience if you must look at the screen. Instead, keep your body positioned toward the audience and move your head to the left (Figure 13.4-v).

Figure 13.4-s Stand Stage Right of Screen

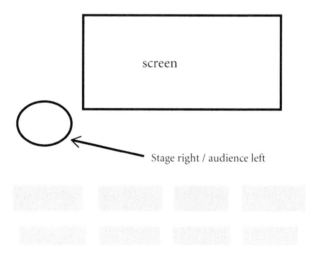

Figure 13.4-t Stand to the Right and Point with Left Arm

Figure 13.4-u Turning Away from the Audience

Figure 13.4-v Point and Glance While Facing the Audience

Sources

Carillo, Frank. "Using Notes in Presentations. Is it okay?" The Total Communicator. Retrieved at http://totalcommunicator.com/vol3_5/expert5.html.

Dempsey, David J. *Legally Speaking: 40 Powerful Presentation Principles Lawyers Need to Know.* New York: Kaplan Publishing, 2009.

Kasperek, Sheila. "Visual Aids." *The Public Speaking Project.* Retrieved from http://publicspeakingproject.org/psvirtualtext.html.

O'Hair, Dan, Hannah Rubenstein, and Rob Stewart. *A Pocket Guide to Public Speaking.* 2016. New York: Bedford/St. Martin's, 2016.

Reiffenstein, Kathy. "Blog on Creating Confident Persuasive Speakers." Retrieved from http://andnowpresenting.typepad.com/professionally_speaking/.

Part Three

Types of Speeches

Chapter 14: The Informative Speech

Chapter 15: The Persuasive Speech

Chapter 16: The Question and Answer Session

Chapter 17: Media Interviews and Press Conferences

Chapter 18: The Special Occasion Speech

Chapter 14

The Informative Speech

Informative speeches are the type that you'll present most often with the purpose of educating your audience. In these speeches, you will describe and explain legally significant concepts, doctrines, events, controversies, and issues. Also, you will demonstrate legally significant processes.

Informative speaking offers excellent opportunities to market yourself and your practice to potential clients. Teaching lay audiences about legal topics that are relevant to their lives and businesses provides an excellent service and demonstrates your expertise, strengthening your reputation in the community.

Informative speaking can strengthen your reputation in the profession as well. Presenting Continuing Legal Education sessions, providing workshops to colleagues in your firm, and speaking at bar functions all increase your profile in the legal community.

Do not use the informative speech to advocate or prompt your listeners to change their attitudes or to take action. Approach the topic objectively and, in the role of "teacher," provide information in an unbiased way. Leave it up to the listeners to use the information as they see fit.

14.1 Organization

Use an appropriate organizational arrangement. Use the principles in Chapter 4 to select the arrangement that will most effectively and logically communicate the information.

- The Chronological Arrangement should be used when speaking about current or historical events, life stories, and in demonstrations.

- The Topical Arrangement works well for complicated topics that involve several independent points.

- The Advantages and Disadvantages Arrangement (Compare-Contrast Arrangement) allows you to show how two or more things are similar or different.

- The Cause and Effect Arrangement identifies a certain situation (cause) and then describes the response (effect).

- The Spatial Arrangement should be used when you are describing the configuration of the parts or levels of a structure, place, system, or object.

- The Problem-Solution Arrangement is most often used in persuasive speeches but can also be used in informative speaking to objectively describe a problem and the solution developed to address it.

14.2 Audience Awareness

You will speak to two types of audiences—listeners without legal training (lay audiences) and lawyers. Regardless of the audience type, your listeners must be able to process the information, and trust that you are credible and knowledgeable about the topic.

A. Presenting Legal Topics to a Lay Audience

Assume that members of a lay audience are unfamiliar with legal doctrine and processes. The material will be new to them, often confusing, and difficult to understand. Your approach should always be to "keep it simple."

1. Using plain language, define and explain legal terms of art and jargon. Recall how you needed to look up almost every word in the cases you were reading during the early days of your first year in law school. Those are the terms that you most certainly should define.

2. If a term isn't significant, use a simpler word instead. For instance, rather than saying, "The appellate court entered a writ of mandamus requiring the lower court to …" say, "The appellate court ordered the trial court to …" Instead of saying, "The Supreme Court granted cert …" say, "The Supreme Court agreed to hear the case."

3. Relate and compare technical information to things that audience members are familiar with.

4. Stay "out of the weeds." You won't have the time, and the audience won't have the stamina to absorb intricate concepts in one sitting. Cover the fundamentals during the speech and provide a handout *after* the presentation that treats the topic in depth.

5. Consider different learning styles. The audience will include listeners with a variety of learning styles—aural and visual being the two most common. Visual learners will respond well to visual aids that explain the point you are making—charts, diagrams, photographs. Aural learners benefit from audio visual aids and explicit explanations of your point.

6. Audience members will have gained much of their "knowledge" and formed their impressions about law, lawyers, and legal processes from exposure to popular culture. Unfortunately, movies, television programs, and novels develop misconceptions in your listeners' minds about these. Be alert to and address any misconceptions that are relevant to your topic.

B. Presenting Legal Topics to Lawyers

You can assume that the lawyers in your audience will be familiar with the basics. Don't assume, however, that they have expert-level knowledge about all legal topics and principles.

1. Be mindful of the practice areas and experience levels of the lawyers attending your speech.

2. Lawyers are often insecure in these situations, because they do not want to appear to be "stupid." Therefore, they may be reluctant to participate, to contribute to the sessions, or to ask questions.

3. If you are presenting a continuing legal education session, be careful to relate new information to information that the lawyers have already learned.

14.3 The Importance of Supporting Evidence

As described in detail in Chapter 15, your points must be supported by strong evidence gathered from well-informed, unbiased sources. Not only must you trust these sources, but your audience must consider them to be credible and reliable. Cite to these sources as you speak.

Sources

O'Hair, Dan, Hannah Rubenstein, and Rob Stewart. *A Pocket Guide to Public Speaking.* 2016. New York: Bedford/St. Martin's, 2016.

Schreiber, Lisa. "Informative Speaking." *The Public Speaking Project.* Retrieved from http://publicspeakingproject.org/psvirtualtext.html.

Chapter 15

The Persuasive Speech

You may think that training to be a trial or appellate lawyer gives you all the skills that you need to be a persuasive speaker. Not true—well at least not completely true. As this text has shown, public speaking is different from advocating in court. The basic principles of persuasion apply to both, but there are important strategies that are different in the public speaking context.

Audiences for your persuasive speeches will be different than the judges and juries in the courtroom. You will speak to legislative committees, administrative agencies, city and county commissions, politically-active civic organizations, unions, and average citizens.

The topics you will address and the results that you seek will be different as well. Rather than advocating for a verdict or judicial decision, you will be urging your audience to adopt your point of view regarding a policy or controversy. You may be encouraging your audience to take actions such as passing or rejecting legislation, a regulation, or an ordinance. You may be persuading your audience to lobby for or against legislation or to vote for a particular candidate.

15.1 Audience Awareness (Chapter 2)

The success of a persuasive speech hinges on your audience analysis. You will encounter receptive, unreceptive (hostile), or neutral audiences. It is essential that you use the techniques covered in Chapter 2 to determine what type of audience you'll be facing. Each category requires tailored persuasive strategies and an appropriate organizational arrangement for you to achieve your speech's persuasive goals.

A. Receptive

Receptive listeners are on your side. They understand the topic and are sympathetic to your position about it. Most likely, they agree that some action should be taken.

Don't focus your speech on convincing them that the topic is important or that it's relevant to them. Start by reminding them about your common interest and opinion about the topic and then tell them what you want them to do. Most of your work in the speech will be to convince them that your solution is the correct one.

B. Unreceptive (Hostile)

Unreceptive listeners don't agree that there is a problem to be addressed, don't agree that it is relevant, and don't agree with your position about it. They may very well believe that the situation is a good one rather than a problem. They will not, therefore, agree that any action need be taken or that the action you are advocating is the correct one. You can consider these listeners to be hostile if the topic involves an issue that they feel strongly about, and they feel strongly that your position opposes theirs.

Be realistic about what you hope to achieve with the speech to these listeners. The most that you can expect when presenting a persuasive speech to them is that they will be moved either to agree that you *may* be correct or that they will agree to consider your position's merits.

It would not be realistic, for example, to expect members of the American Association for Justice (formerly Association of Trial Lawyers of America) to support legislation that would place caps on non-economic damages in medical negligence cases. You might, however, persuade them to agree that reasonable efforts should be considered to develop methods for more accurately evaluating the value of pain and suffering in these cases. It would not be realistic to expect members of Mothers Against Drunk Driving to support legislation making a first-time conviction for drunk driving punishable only by a traffic ticket. It might be reasonable, however, to persuade them to consider whether methods other than imprisonment would deter drunk driving.

Do not assert your position or your call to action at the beginning of your speech. This will alienate the unreceptive audience. For example, if speaking to MADD, you would not lead the speech by saying that the punishment for a first-time DUI conviction should only be punished with a traffic ticket.

Instead, establish common ground by identifying the areas where you agree. For example, when speaking to MADD members, first establish that you agree that drunk driving is a serious problem and that you agree with the organization's mission to end drunk and drugged driving. Then explain that you and MADD believe that criminal punishment is one method to achieve its goal. Once you've established this common ground, you would move on to your point that incarceration is only one form of punishment and that others are available that will work to deter drunk driving. You would present evidence that supports your point that imprisonment is not always the best approach.

Then recognize their point of view and how it opposes yours. Don't directly attack their point of view by saying that it is "wrong." Instead, characterize the audience's beliefs as misconceptions about your point of view. Recognize that these misconceptions are reasonable, but refute them using credible, accurate support. Only then should you identify your goal.

C. Neutral

You will often speak to an audience that is indifferent to or uniformed about the topic and, therefore, has no opinion about it. Your primary goal when speaking to neutral listeners is to convince them that your proposition is important and relevant to them. To accomplish this, you first must capture the listeners' attention and arouse their interest in the topic (Chapter 5).

Next, remind them of beliefs about the topic that you have in common. Then show them that the topic is relevant to them by convincing them that it has a direct impact on them or on people they care about.

Realistically, the most that you may be able to accomplish with a neutral audience is to arouse interest and recognition that the topic is significant. Expecting audience members to take immediate action will be unrealistic, because it's too early. People who have just learned about a problem usually are not ready to address it. You can offer them your solution and explain its merits, but don't focus on moving them to take action.

D. Combination

It won't be unusual for you to speak to an audience that is a combination of the three audience types. If you can determine the degree to which each group is represented, craft and present the speech aiming at the group composing the largest number of listeners. If, however, you are not certain about how the audience is composed, lean toward crafting and presenting the speech to an unreceptive audience.

15.2 Methods (Theories) of Persuasion Outside the Courtroom

As with persuasion in the courtroom, speaking persuasively outside the courtroom employs rule based and analogical reasoning, as well as appeals focused on policy and custom. The persuasive methods derive from the classic strategies Aristotle explained in "The Art of Rhetoric." On the surface they may seem abstract and academic, but they have very important practical applications. In fact, all persuasive messages in advertising, in political speeches, and in pleas to parents, spouses, teachers, and friends use these methods even when the speaker isn't consciously or intentionally employing them. Your persuasive speeches will be most effective in getting results if you purposefully apply them when speaking.

A. Ethos

Establish credibility with your audience. Your listeners must believe and trust you before they will agree with you or take the action you seek.

Just the fact that you are a lawyer will convey authority to some audiences. Unfortunately, others will have the opposite perception because of the negative reputation that lawyers often suffer. Don't merely rely on your role as lawyer to win your audience's belief and trust.

Your appearance and delivery will be critical. Pay attention to the first impression that you establish. Of course, your appearance and demeanor must be professional. Ensure that you are introduced properly. When you've been introduced, approach the stage and lectern with confidence. Throughout the speech maintain your enthusiasm, but be genuine. Your audience will easily detect insincerity.

Your speech's content will also support your credibility. Identify and underscore the beliefs and values that you share with your listeners. Support your points with accurate statistics, data, and examples gleaned from reliable, credible sources.

B. Logos

This is the reasoning method most familiar to lawyers—the use of logic to lead the audience to the conclusion. Typically, this involves the application of the Toulmin Model, inductive reasoning, and deductive reasoning.

The Toulmin model is considered the classic structure of logical reasoning. The speaker asserts a claim, grounds, and a warrant. For example:

Claim: This legislature should enact legislation requiring that all judges in the state be appointed by the governor rather than elected by the state's voters.

Ground: Judges appointed by the governor were the subject of 70% fewer conflict of interest cases than were judges elected by the voters.

Warrant: Appointing, rather than electing, judges will decrease the number of judicially related conflict of interest cases in the state.

Using inductive reasoning, you describe several specific examples that lead to and support a general claim. For example:

Specific instances:
In 2015, five elected judges were the subject of conflict of interest cases, and one judge appointed by the governor was the subject of a conflict of interest case. In 2016, seven elected judges were the subject of conflict of interest cases, and two judges appointed by the governor were the subject of conflict of interest cases.

General Claim:
In 2017, there will be fewer cases of conflict of interest involving judges appointed by the governor than conflict of interest cases involving elected judges.

Deductive reasoning, or syllogistic reasoning (major premise, minor premise, conclusion), involves using a general proposition to support a conclusion about a specific instance. For example:

All judges elected by the voters become the subject of conflict of interest cases. (Major Premise)

Alvin Topper is a judge elected by the voters. (Minor Premise)

Alvin Topper will become the subject of a conflict of interest case. (Conclusion)

Avoid the common fallacies in logic. Demonstrate the validity of your logic by using credible, accurate data.

C. Pathos

People are strongly influenced by appeals to sympathy, passion, empathy, compassion, fear, policy, values, and prejudice. Evoke these emotions in your listeners using compelling stories and dramatic examples. Be sure, however, that these stories and examples are plausible and genuine. An audience that feels manipulated will not be moved.

15.3 Format and Organizational Considerations

In addition to the Comparative Advantages and Problem-Solution arrangements described in Chapter 4, there are three other effective approaches to organizing persuasive speeches.

A. Monroe's Motivated Sequence

Alan H. Monroe, a communications professor at Purdue, developed this approach for organizing an effective persuasive speech. He used principles of the psychology of persuasion to create this sequence of steps that have formed the structure of successful advertisements and political speeches.

1. Attention

Grab your audience's attention in your opening (Chapter 5).

2. Need

Demonstrate to your audience that there is a problem (need) that requires attention. Use statistics, examples, and other support to prove that the problem is real and that it directly affects them.

3. Satisfaction

Propose your solution to the problem. Provide a detailed explanation of the solution and show how it will satisfy the need. Use data, examples and other support to prove that it will be effective.

4. Visualization

Using concrete, realistic examples, have the audience visualize the consequences of allowing the problem to continue. You can also have the audience visualize the positive results of adopting your solution.

5. Action

Concluding your speech, prompt your listeners to take action. Provide specific actions that your listeners can take to implement your solution.

B. Direct Method Arrangement

This approach is simple and effective in persuading the audience to adopt a particular idea. State the idea and then describe reasons supporting your assertion that the idea has merit. This technique will not be effective, however, if the audience is unreceptive to your message.

C. Refutation Arrangement

This arrangement can be used when your goal is to convince an unreceptive audience that your position about an issue is correct and is sounder than its opposing argument. First, identify the audience's argument that you will refute. Then assert your position and provide support for its merit.

15.4 The Importance of Supporting Evidence

A. Support Your Points with Examples, Statistics, and Stories

To persuade an audience, your assertions must be supported by strong evidence. This evidence must come from reliable, credible sources that your audience will trust.

Obtain this material from sources that are well-informed and unbiased about the topic.

For example, the Flat Earth Society probably would not represent a credible source of scientific data. Analyze the audience to determine which sources your listeners will consider to be reliable. For example, members of the Federalist Society might not trust information gleaned from The Carter Center as much as they would trust information provided by The American Enterprise Institute. Results of a study on traffic safety by the National Highway Traffic Safety Administration might carry more weight than research results provided by the Alliance of Automobile Manufacturers.

> **A word of caution**: Don't trust everything that you find on the internet. The ease of online research can lead you to websites that are not trustworthy. Before relying on information published on a website that isn't sponsored by a known and trusted individual or entity, evaluate its credibility. Consider the following points:

- What is the website's purpose and who is its intended audience?
- Is an author (individual or organization) identified and the author's credentials listed?
- Does the author provide contact information?
- Does the website have a trustworthy URL—.org, .edu, .gov., .net?
- Is the date the site was created current?
- Is the date that the information was gathered indicated?
- Is the factual information contained on the website attributed with correct citations to reliable sources?
- Does the information agree with other information that you've gathered?
- Does the information seem reasonable to you?

B. Cite to the Sources of the Information

Do this in a way that fits the flow of your speech and that sounds natural.

According to a 2017 study by the National Highway Traffic Safety Administration …

Or

In 2017, the National Highway Traffic Safety Administration revealed …

Or

In a recent interview on CNN, Professor Mark Smith, author of the book, Automobiles—Killers on the Road, said that …

Provide citations to sources of information and photographs included in slideware presentations. Include the citation on the relevant slide.

15.5 Special Considerations for Openings and Closings

Overall, openings and closings in persuasive speeches should be crafted according to the principles discussed in Chapter 5 but with the following modifications:

A. Openings

1. In addition to introducing the topic, clearly introduce the problem or your proposition.

2. Relate the problem/proposition to the audience.

3. If the audience is receptive or neutral, identify the solution that you are advocating or the action you want the audience to take. *Never* do this if the audience is unreceptive.

B. Closings

If the audience is receptive or neutral, include a call to action. Vividly tell the audience what you want it to do.

Sources

Dempsey, David J. *Legally Speaking: 40 Powerful Presentation Principles Lawyers Need to Know*. New York: Kaplan Publishing, 2009.

"Monroe's Motivated Sequence." Retrieved from http://changingminds.org/techniques/general/overall/monroe_sequence.htm.

Reiffenstein, Kathy. "Blog on Creating Confident Persuasive Speakers." Retrieved from http://andnowpresenting.typepad.com/professionally_speaking/.

Chapter 16

The Question and Answer Session

The question and answer session is an important part of the entire presentation, because it creates the last impression that you leave with the audience. It's not the time to "relax." Treat it with the same care as you did the speech – employ all delivery techniques and remember, the presentation does not end until you leave the stage.

Often speakers are more anxious about the question and answer session than about presenting the speech. The speaker fears appearing to be uninformed when not knowing the answer to the questions and fears giving control to the audience. Also, there's always the fear that audience members will have no questions, creating the impression that they were not engaged in the presentation.

There are techniques for avoiding all these problems and ensuring that the Q&A session will provide a strong ending to the presentation and will build a relationship between you and the audience.

A. Preparing for the Q&A Session

1. Most speaking occasions will allow time for the audience to ask you questions. Confirm with your host the amount of time allotted to your entire presentation and then, while practicing, determine how much time your speech will consume and leave the rest for questions and answers.

2. Anticipate questions that are likely to be asked and develop answers. Conduct a brainstorming session to generate questions that may arise.

3. Practice the Q&A session when practicing your speech in front of an audience of friends and colleagues. Review the recording and refine answers to the questions raised during the practice.

4. To anticipate difficult or hostile questions, pretend that you can send your host a list of questions that you don't want the audience to ask. List and prepare for them.

B. Conducting the Q&A Session

1. Take questions at the end of the presentation.

Conduct the question and answer session after the speech. Avoid taking questions during the speech, because they will interrupt the flow and take you off track. One question will lead to another, the audience will take control, and the speech will become disjointed. Ultimately, you'll have the unwelcome choice of either cutting off the questions or giving up on the speech.

2. Dedicate at least five minutes to the session.

Allow at least five minutes for the Q&A session. If you have gone over the allotted time and you have less than five minutes, don't take questions. Make yourself available after the speech to chat with the audience. You can give out your card and encourage audience members to contact you via email.

3. Start the Q&A session after the applause.

Conclude your speech, enjoy the applause, and then tell the audience that you have time for questions. Let the audience know how much time will be allotted for the session.

4. Get the ball rolling by asking, "What questions do you have?"[3]

This question presumes that audience members have questions. It seems as though you are begging for questions when you ask, "Are there any questions?"

5. Have a pre-arranged question ready.

The beginning of the Q&A can be awkward when audience members are shy about asking questions. No one wants to be the first. In many respects,

---

3. Dempsey, David J. Legally Speaking: 40 Powerful Presentation Principles Lawyers Need to Know. New York: Kaplan Publishing, 2009.

asking a question is public speaking, and, as you know, everyone is afraid to speak publically.

To avoid the awkward silence, pre-arrange with someone in the audience to ask the first question. Pre-arranging a question is useful because, first, you know the question and will have an answer ready. Second, once the ice has been broken, more questions will follow.

6. Don't point your finger at audience members (Figure 16-a).

Instead, use an open hand "point" (Figure 16-b) when recognizing someone having a question.

Figure 16-a Don't Point

Figure 16-b Open Hand Point

7. Repeat the questions (except hostile questions — see #13 below).

Repeat the question before answering. Even when an audience member uses a microphone, some may not have heard it. Repeating the question also ensures that you understood it and gives you time to formulate an answer.

When repeating the question, say, "The question was . . ." rather than, "He asked the question. . ." etc.

8. Treat every question as a "good one."

Avoid saying, "That's a good question." All audience members consider their questions to be good ones. Otherwise, they would not take the chance of asking them.

9. There are no "stupid" questions.

Few, if any, audience members think that their questions are stupid. Regardless of how ridiculous you think a question may be, do not react that way. Instead, answer it as respectfully as you do all questions.

Also, be careful when reacting to what you think is a humorous question. The questioner may not have intended the question to be "funny" and will be offended if you treat it that way.

10. Maintain eye contact with the entire audience while answering the question.

Start by looking at the questioner, then scan around the room as you speak. This will keep the audience engaged and will encourage more questions.

11. Don't fake it if you don't understand the question or don't know the answer.

If you don't understand the question you should try to paraphrase it and ask the questioner if that is what the question was. Don't say, "I don't understand the question, can you repeat it?" Place the burden on yourself rather than the audience member.

If you still can't figure out what the question is, apologize and tell the audience member that you'd be happy to chat after the session.

If you don't know the answer to a question, be honest and say so. Then ask to chat after the session so that you can offer to research the question and "get back" to the audience member later.

12. Don't be flustered by a pause in questions.

If there's a lull in questions, pause a moment, remain calm, smile, and look around. Give audience members a few moments to gather their thoughts and courage to ask another question. After a few moments say "what other questions do you have?" If none, then conclude.

13. Keep your cool when asked hostile questions.

Although audience members may take issue with a point mentioned in the speech, they rarely will challenge you maliciously. So don't take it personally. If, however, an audience member, for whatever reason, attacks you personally, your reaction is crucial. If you keep your temper and don't take the bait, the bad behavior will reflect on the audience member and not on you. If you become defensive and lose your temper, the audience will sympathize with the questioner and will lose respect for you. Do not repeat the question, but instead, rephrase it in a positive manner, answer it concisely, and move on.

14. Keep track of time.

When you see that you are almost out of time, announce that you have time for one more question.

15. Conclude the session with a "bang."

Treat the end of the Q&A session as the conclusion of the entire presentation. Provide a powerful closing similar to the one you used at the end of the speech. Have this conclusion memorized as you did for the one closing the speech.

Sources

Dempsey, David J. *Legally Speaking: 40 Powerful Presentation Principles Lawyers Need to Know.* New York: Kaplan Publishing, 2009.

Detz, Joan. *Can You Say a Few Words?* New York: St. Martin's Griffin, 2006.

O'Hair, Dan, Hannah Rubenstein, and Rob Stewart. *A Pocket Guide to Public Speaking,* 2016. New York: Bedford/St. Martin's, 2016.

Chapter 17

Media Interviews and Press Conferences

If you represent well-known clients or are involved in high-profile litigation or transactions, you may be called upon to speak to the public through news media. This form of public speaking requires some unique preparation and delivery methods and raises important ethical concerns that typically are not involved in the other public speaking situations.

As with any situation where you represent a client, you must adhere to your state's rules of professional responsibility. Speaking to the press, however, requires attention to special rules, especially when discussing a case in litigation. ABA Model Rule 3.6 Trial Publicity, adopted in one form or another by most states, provides the conditions under which you may and may not speak about a trial. Of course, rules regarding confidentiality always apply.

Be Careful—Despite a reporter's assurances to the contrary, consider that nothing you say is "off the record." Do not tell a reporter anything that you do not want to see in print or repeated on television and radio.

17.1 Have a Purpose

Never conduct a press conference or submit to an interview unless you have a good reason for doing so. The prime reason should always be to help your client in some way. Use these opportunities to give your client's side of the story, set the facts straight from your client's perspective, and educate the public and the press.

17.2 Have a Message

The first step in preparing for interviews and press conferences is to develop the message that you want to convey. Explore the things that you need to say in order to achieve your goals for helping your client and condense them into a theme. Use the theme (similar to a litigator's "theory of the case") to craft the messages that best underscore and communicate that theme.

17.3 Prepare

A. Anticipate the Questions

Before the press conference or interview, brainstorm with your colleagues about likely questions, and craft answers that will place your client in a positive light and will express your message.

Prepare for the difficult questions first. The best way to anticipate problem questions is to pretend that you could give the reporter a list of questions that may not be asked because they are harmful to your client and you want to avoid answering them. Make the list and craft the best possible answer for each. Although you may not be able to formulate a "home run" answer for each of these questions, you will have thought about them and will be ready to provide a response that's better than stammering with a "deer in the headlights" look on your face. Quite possibly, after thinking through the problem questions, you may find that your client's position isn't as weak as you first thought and that you can, in fact, drive a stake into the heart of the problem.

After you've addressed the problem questions, anticipate and prepare answers for the others.

B. Practice

Just as you would for a speech (Chapter 6), conduct several practice sessions. These practice sessions should be mock interviews or press conferences in which your colleagues play the role of the reporters posing the questions that you've prepared for.

Record these practice sessions. Review the recording to evaluate the quality of your responses and, as needed, fine tune your answers. During these sessions, you'll encounter additional questions that had not been considered during the brainstorming process.

If you are preparing for a press conference or broadcast interview, use the recordings to evaluate and refine your delivery techniques.

17.4 Answering the Questions during the Interview or Press Conference

A. Be Concise

Keep your answers succinct and to the point. If you ramble during an answer, you are more likely to say something that isn't helpful to your clients. Follow the advice that lawyers give their clients when testifying—answer the question asked and no more. Leave it up to the interviewer to draw out the information.

B. Speak to Your Audience

Although good reporters perform extensive research before conducting interviews and know the facts of your client's case and, perhaps, understand the legal issues involved, they are not your audience. Although the reporter asks the questions, the reporter is a surrogate for your actual audience, the people reading the story and viewing the interview or press conference. Therefore, tailor your answers to that audience.

C. Don't Answer What You Don't Know

If you don't know the answer to a question, say so. It's better to admit that you don't know the answer than to make one up. Invariably, the deception will be revealed and your reputation damaged. If the information is important to the story, tell the reporter that you will report back once you've found the answer.

D. Don't Answer What You Don't Understand

Do not answer a question that you do not understand. If you don't understand the question, ask the reporter to clarify it.

E. Answering Difficult/Hostile Questions

When you are asked a difficult, hostile question, do not refuse to answer or say "no comment." If you evade a difficult question, it will appear as though you and your client have something to hide. If you have practiced effectively and have anticipated the "hostile" question, you'll be able to respond effectively.

When you are asked the inevitable hostile question, keep calm, smile, and answer. Anger does not signify strength, so do not allow a reporter's questions to provoke you. If you lose your temper, you will appear weak and out of control. What's worse, you will not be able to think clearly and formulate effective answers. Rather than give thoughtful answers, you'll say things that you and your client won't want to read, hear, or watch later.

Use the Bridge/Pivot Technique as an effective way to protect your client when a direct and honest answer will be harmful or will reveal weaknesses in your client's case. This type of response recasts the question to be helpful to your client. While appearing to be answering the question directly, bridge to a response that is related to the question's topic but, instead, reinforces your message and places your client in a positive light.

For example, a reporter asks a lawyer representing XYA, Inc., a manufacturing company,

> *"How can your client's CEO justify the 30% pay gap between men and women doing the same jobs in the company's factory and the fact that he is earning 350 times more than what the highest paid worker in the company's factory makes?"*

Using the Bridge/Pivot Technique, the lawyer responds,

> *"Well, that statistic is concerning, but you've got to recognize that Mr. Franaca values all the men and women working in his factory. In fact, he's proud that since he took over as CEO, overall worker satisfaction at XYA has increased and continues to rise. In a recent report, the benefits packages, working conditions, attention to comfort and safety, were all rated to be the best in the industry."*

This technique is a favorite of politicians. It does a good job of avoiding the question but has the danger of annoying the reporter and the audience.

17.5 Expect the Unexpected— The Ambush Interview

Don't allow yourself to be a victim of the reporter lurking outside the courthouse who ambushes you with questions when you have not planned or prepared for an interview. You should never be "surprised" by these encounters.

If you are involved in a highly-publicized case or transaction, you must anticipate that the press will seek you out and try to catch you off guard. Therefore, always be prepared for these encounters and ready for obvious questions that will arise.

When ambushed, remain composed and do not try to avoid the reporter or the question. Answer the question as briefly and concisely as you can and then say that you must go. Offer to "sit down" with the reporter at another time and suggest that the reporter contact your office to schedule an interview.

17.6 Delivery Techniques for Broadcast Interviews and Press Conferences

Broadcast interviews and press conferences require attention to your delivery mechanics as well as to the content of your answers. Use delivery techniques that will engage your audience and will enhance rather than distract from your client's message.

A. Broadcast Interviews

Broadcast interviews usually take place in two forms. You will either be interviewed in a studio in the presence of the interviewer, or you will be interviewed while at a studio that is remote from the interviewer's studio. During the remote interview, you will be supplied with an earpiece so that you can hear the questions, and you will sit facing a camera. A monitor showing the interviewer or the "split screen" view shown to the audience may also be available.

In addition to the delivery techniques and audience awareness considerations covered throughout this text, observe the following guidelines:

1. Sit comfortably but don't slouch.

2. Keep your hands and arms still. Gestures do not read well on television.

3. If you are in the studio, look at the interviewer not the camera or monitor.

4. If you are at a remote location, maintain "eye contact" with the camera, looking directly at the lens. This will give the impression that you are looking at the interviewer and audience.

5. Pause a few seconds before answering a question. This will ensure that you won't interrupt if the interviewer hasn't finished talking. This is especially important during remote interviews.

6. Don't let technical problems fluster you. If, for example, you lose audio contact with the interviewer during a remote interview, calmly say that you can't hear the questions, and then wait for the technicians to fix the problem. The audience understands that technical problems are not your fault and will admire your unruffled reaction.

B. Press Conferences

Even if not broadcast "live," you should expect that the press conference will be recorded for television and radio broadcast.

1. Schedule, plan, and prepare for the press conference. Never conduct impromptu press conferences.

2. Make a brief opening statement that will establish your message. This will also reinforce the topic that you want to cover and avoid your being sidetracked.

3. Stay in control.

   • Establish and keep to an announced time limit.

   • Require the reporters to raise hands rather than call out questions.

   • Expect that some reporters will try to grab the spotlight by grand-standing. Don't let them provoke your anger.

4. Unlike in a question and answer session after a speech, do not repeat the questions.

5. Maintain eye contact with all the reporters in the room while you speak. Scan the audience while answering a question rather than limiting your gaze to the reporter asking the question. Don't look at the cameras recording the session.

Sources

Call, Michael D. "A Lawyer's Guide to News Media Interviews." *Law Prac. Mgmt.*, May/June.

O'Hair, Dan, Hannah Rubenstein, and Rob Stewart. *A Pocket Guide to Public Speaking.* 2016. New York: Bedford/St. Martin's, 2016.

Chapter 18

The Special Occasion Speech

18.1 Types of Special Occasion Speeches

As a lawyer, you will attend a variety of events related to the profession, and you'll be asked to speak. You'll be asked to speak at social functions as well, often because people think that because you are a lawyer, you enjoy public speaking and are good at it.

The typical types of these speeches:

- Introductions

- Speeches commemorating an event

- Eulogies

- Speeches honoring a person, group, or organization

- Speeches roasting someone

- Presenting and Getting Awards

- Toasts (usually wedding toasts)

18.2 General Considerations

With some modifications, these speeches should be prepared and presented just like any other speech. Follow the organizational patterns discussed in Chapter 4. Generally, keep the following tips in mind:

A. Keep It Short and Sweet

Speak for only five to ten minutes.

B. It's Not about You

Speak about the person, organization or event that you are honoring, commemorating, or roasting, not about yourself.

C. Show, Don't Tell

Use stories that highlight the honoree's successes, values, and qualities. For example, rather than merely saying that "Judge Parker loved his family," tell the story about how he took his parents on their "bucket list" trip to the Grand Canyon rather than spending his much needed vacation skiing in North Carolina. Instead of saying that "Edna was a great lawyer," tell stories about some of her best cases and refer to her notable accomplishments. Do not, however, merely present an "oral resume."

D. Balance Sentiment with Humor, Carefully

Include humor that is appropriate and suitable for the occasion. Tell lighthearted stories, gently tease, but never embarrass the honoree, family, or guests. If you have any doubt about telling a story, leave it out.

18.3 Some Special Delivery Considerations

A. Wedding Toasts

1. Stay away from the open bar and strictly limit your alcohol consumption until after you give the toast.

2. Think about the toast as a wedding gift to the bride and groom. Even though you will be speaking to the guests as well as the wedding party, your primary audience will be the bride and groom. The guests will forget the toast by the time the wedding cake is served, but the couple will remember it for many years, and, most likely, for life, if it's recorded.

3. Mix humor and sentiment to make the couple and guests laugh and cry.

4. When using humor:

    •   Although humor is an important ingredient, use it sparingly. The toast is not a way to impress the guests with your talent as a stand-up comedian.

    •   Avoid using inside jokes that are funny only to you and the couple.

    •   Do not, under any circumstances, mention former boyfriends and girlfriends.

    •   Keep the jokes clean. You don't want to offend Grandma, Grandpa, Mom, Dad, and Aunt Ethel.

5. Stick to the traditional. Although the guests may be impressed with how creative and witty you are if your toast is unconventional, the couple might be disappointed that you didn't give them a traditional, heartfelt toast.

6. The toast should be no longer than five minutes.

7. Look at the couple as well the guests during the toast.

8. Wedding reception guests can be a rowdy group, so be prepared for mayhem during your toast. Guests will talk, babies will cry, and plates and silverware will clatter. Don't let the atmosphere fluster you.

Organizing the Traditional Wedding Toast

•   Start off by using stories to describe what type of person your friend/brother/sister is.

•   Next, move on to talking about your friend/brother/sister meeting the bride/groom.

•   Then, describe how your friend/brother/sister is even more wonderful because of the bride/groom.

•   Close by saying how happy you are that the bride and groom are together.

B. The Eulogy

This is the most difficult of the special occasion speeches, because the occasion is solemn, and the audience and you are grieving. The best approach is to be gentle in demeanor.

1. Your primary audience is the immediate family.

2. The eulogy should be no longer than five minutes.

3. The eulogy is about the deceased, not about you and how the death has affected you. Speak in terms of how everyone was affected by the deceased's life as well as death.

4. Tell stories that illustrate uplifting memories, the deceased's qualities and the deceased's values. These stories can focus on such things as the deceased's significant accomplishments, childhood memories, favorite pastimes, work life, etc. However, don't chronicle the deceased's entire life.

5. Humor is acceptable so long as it is relevant, appropriate, and limited.

How to Deal with Becoming Emotional during the Eulogy

- It's very likely that at some point during the eulogy, you will become emotional. It's natural and perfectly acceptable, so don't apologize if you do.

- To avoid losing your composure, speak slowly, take pauses, and breathe deeply.

- Have a bottle of water available. If you sense that you are becoming too emotional, pause and sip some water.

- Maintain eye contact with friends in the audience on whom you rely for strength and composure.

- Have a back-up person ready to take over if you are unable to finish the eulogy.

Sources

Detz, Joan. *Can You Say a Few Words?* New York: St. Martin's Griffin, 2006.
Pennebaker, Teal. "Ten Maid of Honor Speech Ideas &Tips to Help You Give a Killer Toast." Retrieved from https://www.brides.com/story/maid-of-honor-toast-tips.

Appendix

Checklists

Use these checklists to guide your preparation, presentation, and evaluation of your speeches.

Part One:
The Basics

Controlling and Surviving Public Speaking Anxiety

❑ Techniques to control anxiety

- Accept anxiety as a natural response to public speaking.

- Don't be anxious about being nervous.

- Use square breathing to become calm.

- Act self-assured.

- Interact with audience members before the speech.

- Take deep breaths to control a shaky voice.

- Stay hydrated to relieve a dry mouth.

- Prepare and practice to be confident.

❑ Things to avoid

- Don't imagine audience members naked or sitting on the toilet.

- Don't avoid eye contact with audience members.
- Don't consume alcohol or take sedatives before the speech.

Know Your Audience

<u>The information that you need to know</u>

❑ What are the demographics and psychological profiles of audience members?

- Age and "generational identity"
- Gender
- Income
- Religion
- Political affiliations
- Group Affiliations

❑ What is the depth of audience members' knowledge about the topic?

- Lay audience members are not familiar with legal principles and processes.
- Legally-trained audience members are familiar with basic legal principles but are not experts about all legal principles and processes.

❑ What is the audience's motivation for attending the speech?

- Are audience members attending voluntarily?
- Are the listeners a captive audience?

❑ What is the audience's attitude about the topic?

- Receptive
  - Audience members are interested in the topic, eager to listen, and agree with your point of view.
- Neutral
  - Audience members are indifferent or uninformed about the topic.
- Unreceptive (hostile)
  - Audience members do not agree with your point of view about the topic.
- Combination

- – Audience is comprised of a mixture of receptive, neutral, and unreceptive listeners.

❑ What is the "identity" of the organization or legislative body?

- • Civic groups, clubs, associations

- • Legislative committees, city councils, county commissions

How to find the information

❑ Interview the host.

❑ Interview audience members.

❑ Use the internet.

❑ Use a questionnaire.

Organizing Your Speech

❑ The large-scale organization of the speech should contain the following elements:

- • Introduction

- • Body

- • Conclusion

❑ Use a cohesive structure for the main points in the body of the speech.

- • Chronological Arrangement

- • Topical Arrangement

- • Advantages and Disadvantages Arrangement (Compare-Contrast Arrangement)

- • Cause and Effect Arrangement

- • Spatial Arrangement

- Problem-Solution Arrangement

❑ Use transitions to guide your listeners and show them the relationships between the main points.

- Signal that you are moving from the introduction to the speech's body.

- Show a progression from point to point.

- Link sections demonstrating contrasting or similar points.

- Link points demonstrating cause and effect.

- Signal that you are moving from the body of the speech to the conclusion.

❑ Prefer categorizing and conveying the information in no more than three main points.

Openings and Closings

Opening

❑ Gain audience's attention and interest.

- Surprising Statistic

- Shocking statement

- Quotation

- Rhetorical Question or Survey Question

- Enthralling Story

- Humor

- Visual or Audio Aid

❑ Introduce the topic clearly and relate it to the audience.

❑ Provide a clear road map or preview to the speech.

<u>Closing</u>

❑ Employ a vivid closing method.

- • Bookend Closing

- • Challenge Closing

- • Echo Closing

- • Callback Closing

- • Quotation Closing

❑ Employ an effective structure.

- • Signal that speech is concluding.

- • Summarize the main points.

- • Provide a call to action (persuasive speech).

Productive Practice Sessions

❑ Practice out loud.

❑ Treat practice sessions as dress rehearsals.

❑ Practice with an audience.

❑ Practice with your notes.

❑ Practice with your visual aids.

❑ Record and view the practice sessions.

- • Evaluate and perfect purposeful movements and gestures.

- • Evaluate the speech's organization and content.

❑ Practice at the venue where you will be presenting the speech.

Part Two:
Delivering the Speech
Maintaining a Professional Appearance

❏ You are appearing in your role as an attorney—dress like one.

- Proper attire for men

  - Wear a black, gray, navy, or brown suit.

  - Wear a well-pressed, plain shirt.

  - White is preferred.

  - Wear a conservative, plain tie.

  - Wear black or brown shoes and dark socks.

- Proper attire for women

  - Wear a skirted suit or pantsuit.

  - Wear a blouse with a conservative pattern.

  - Wear conservatively-colored dress shoes or closed-toe heels.

Delivery Mechanics

❏ Maintain good posture.

❏ Convey a strong presence.

- Take command of the stage.

- Prefer speaking without a lectern.

- Keep hands and arms off the lectern.

❏ Use purposeful, planned movements.

❏ Use purposeful, planned gestures.

❏ Maintain strong eye contact with the audience.

❏ Use a purposeful vocal variety and quality.

❏ Eliminate distracting physical and vocal habits

Using Notes

❏ Use notes—don't memorize the speech.

❏ Use key words, quotations, statistics and sources to form the content of your notes.

❏ Use bullet points rather than full sentences.

❏ Use a font size that is easy to read in a glance.

❏ Use a notes system that works best for you.

- Sheets of paper

- Note cards

- Slideware programs and electronic devices

❏ Use PG-EC-RS.

- Pause.

- Glance briefly.

- Regain eye contact.

- Resume speaking.

❏ Practice using your notes.

Using Visual Aids

❏ Use visual aids for the purpose of aiding the speech.

❏ Use appropriate types of visual aids.

- Objects and props

- Handouts

- Photographs

- Flip charts and white boards

- Video and audio

- Slideware presentation programs

❑ Use slideware presentation programs effectively.

- Slide design

  - Text is easy to read.

  - Visible font size.

  - Limited amount of text.

  - Slides are simple and uncluttered.

  - Colors provide contrast between backgrounds and text.

  - Avoids use of "bells and whistles."

  - Charts are easy to digest and understand.

  - Slides are composed using the Rule of Thirds.

  - People and animals are oriented to face slide's center and content.

- Slideware is presented effectively.

  - Appropriate number of slides used.

  - Slides are revealed only when relevant.

  - Audience provided sufficient time to read slide's text.

  - Speaker stands stage right of the slide.

  - Speaker refers to the slides using left arm.

  - Speaker talks to the audience, not the slide.

    - Speaker does not read the slide to the audience.

    - Speaker faces the audience, not the slide.

Part Three: Types of Speeches

Informative Speech

❑ Tailor the presentation to the nature of the audience.

- Lay audience

- Legally trained audience

❑ In the opening

- Clearly introduce the topic.

- Relate the topic to the audience.

- Establish your credibility.

❑ In the body

- Employ an effective organizational arrangement.

  – The Chronological Arrangement

  – The Topical Arrangement

  – The Advantages and Disadvantages Arrangement

  – The Cause and Effect Arrangement

  – The Spatial Arrangement

  – The Problem-Solution Arrangement

- Provide supporting evidence for main points.

- Use sources of supporting evidence that are appropriate for the topic and audience.

Persuasive Speech

❑ Tailor the presentation to the nature of the audience.

- Receptive

- Neutral

- Unreceptive

❑ Use audience motivators.

- Benefits

- Emotions

- Logic

- Values

❑ Use effective types of reasoning.

- Rule Based

- Analogical

- Policy

- Principle

- Custom

❑ In the opening

- Clearly introduce the problem/proposition.

- Relate the problem/proposition to the audience.

- Establish your credibility.

❑ In the body

- Employ an effective organizational pattern:

  – Monroe's Motivated Sequence

  – Direct Method Pattern

  – Causal Pattern

  – Refutation Pattern

- Demonstrate existence of unfulfilled needs (problem).

- Develop an effective/reasonable persuasive purpose/goal.

- Provide supporting evidence for main points.

- Use sources of supporting evidence that are appropriate for the topic and audience.

- Address opposing sides of the issue.
- Propose and argue for a solution/policy.
- Identify and request a specific action.

❑ In the conclusion, provide a "call to action."

Question and Answer Session

❑ Pre-arrange a question with an audience member to "get the ball rolling."

❑ Inform the audience about the amount of time available for questions.

❑ "What questions do you have?"

❑ Use the "open-handed point" when recognizing a questioner.

❑ Repeat the questions.

❑ Maintain control of the room and time.

❑ Signal when there's time for "one more question."

❑ Prepare and use a powerful conclusion.

Media Interviews and Press Conferences

❑ Have a purpose and message to justify talking to the media about your client.

❑ Prepare for interviews and press conferences.

- Anticipate the questions.
- Practice just as you would for a speech.

❑ Answering the questions.

- Be concise.
- Tailor your answers to the audience, not the reporter.
- Don't answer what you don't know.
- Clarify what you don't understand.
- Handle difficult/hostile questions effectively.
  - Keep calm

       – Use the Bridge/Pivot Technique

❑ Expect and prepare for the unexpected—the Ambush Interview.

❑ Use effective delivery mechanics.

- Broadcast interview
  - In studio
    - Avoid distracting gestures.
    - Maintain eye contact with the interviewer.
  - Remote studio
    - Maintain "eye contact" with the camera lens.
    - Pause before answering questions.
    - Don't let technical problems fluster you.
- Press conferences
  - Plan and stay in control.
  - Maintain eye contact with the reporters not the cameras.
  - Expect and handle hostile questions.
  - Don't repeat the questions.

Special Occasion Speech

❑ General considerations for all special occasion speeches.

- Craft and deliver the speech to be about the person, organization, or event that you are honoring, commemorating, or roasting. It isn't about you.
- Use stories to convey your message.
- Use humor with caution.

❑ Additional delivery considerations for specific special occasions.

- Wedding toasts
  - Stay sober before the toast.
  - Craft and deliver the toast with the bride and groom in mind.

- – Use humor with caution.
- – Be traditional.
- – Don't let rowdy guests fluster you.
- Eulogies
  - – The audience is the immediate family.
  - – Speak about the deceased, not about how the death has affected you.
  - – Use stories illustrating uplifting memories about the deceased.
  - – Use humor with caution.
  - – Be prepared to be emotional.

Index

A

anxiety, 3, 5–11
articulation exercises, 95–96
attire, 53–60, 168
attitude and behavior, 54
audience awareness, 13–19, 135, 138, 139
   captive audience, 16, 164
   combination audience, 17, 139, 164, 165
   hostile listeners, 16, 137–138, 148, 151, 155–156, 164, 173
   lay audience, 39, 134–135, 164, 171
   legally trained audience, 15, 39, 135, 164, 171
   neutral audience, 16, 137, 139, 145, 164–165, 171,
   receptive audience, 16, 137–138, 145, 164, 171
   unreceptive audience, 16–17, 137–139, 143, 145, 164–165, 172

B

body movement, 21, 66–70, 99, 105, 168
breathing exercises, 8, 96, 163
broadcast interview, 157–158

C

closing, 43–46, 144–145, 167
   bookend closing, 44, 167
   callback closing, 44, 167
   challenge closing, 44, 167
   echo closing, 44, 167
   quotation closing, 45, 167
   repetitive closing, 44
closing's structure, 26, 45–46, 152, 167

D

demeanor, 54, 162

E

eulogy, 161–162
eye contact, 10, 69–70, 110–111, 152, 159, 163, 165, 169, 175

G

gestures, 22, 49, 72–92, 108
  aggressive point, 76
  air quotation marks, 76
  counting gesture, 73, 79
  cramped counting, 79
  fig leaf, 86
  gesture zone, 77–78
  increase/decrease, 73
  interlocking fingers, 85
  jazz hands, 76–77
  on the other hand, 74
  open hand point, 74, 150
  over-broad, 77–78
  politician thumb-point, 76
  small/medium/large, 73
  thumb-gun pointing, 72
  tiny bit, 74

H

habits, distracting, 97–99
  sing-song pattern, 94
  swaying and rocking, 99
  up-talking, 98
  vocal fillers, 97–98
humor, 41, 160–161, 162, 166, 174, 175

I

informative speech, 29, 133–136, 171

L

logistics, 19–23

M

main and supporting points, developing, 32–34

media interviews, 153–158, 173–174
movement, 66–69, 78, 99, 168
  diamond pattern, 67
  pacing, 67, 99
  point of view, 68–69
  purposeful, 66–70, 99, 169
  swaying, 99
  transitional movement, 66–67

N

notes, 48, 83–84, 101–110, 167, 169
  electronic devices, 108–109, 169
  note card, 21, 84, 103, 105–108, 109, 169
  PG-EC-RS Technique, 109–110, 169
  preparing, 102
  sheet of paper, 102–105, 169

O

opening, 26, 39–43, 144–145, 166
  gain attention, 39–41, 142, 166
    enthralling story, 41, 166
    preview, 42, 166
    rhetorical question, 40, 166
    road map, 42, 166
    shocking statements, 40, 166
    surprising statistic, 40, 166
    survey question, 40
organizational arrangements, 27–31
  Advantages and Disadvantages Arrangement, 28–29, 134, 165
  Cause and Effect Arrangement, 29–30, 134, 166
  Chronological Arrangement, 27–28, 133, 165
  Compare-Contrast Arrangement, 28–29, 134, 165

Direct Method Arrangements, 143, 172

Monroe's Motivated Sequence, 142, 172

Problem-Solution Arrangement, 30–31, 134, 166

Refutation Arrangement, 143, 172

Spatial Arrangement, 30, 134, 165

Topical Arrangement, 28, 134, 165

outline, 35–37

P

persuasion methods, 140–142
  Ethos, 140
  Logos, 140–141
  Pathos, 141–142
  Toulmin Model, 140–141

persuasive speech, 29, 137–145, 171–173

posture, 61–63

practice sessions, 47–49, 167

presence, 64–66, 168

press conference, 153–155, 158, 173–174

Q

Question and Answer Sessions, 22, 147–152, 173

R

ready position, 81–92

relaxed-formal air, 54, 60

S

setting and context, 19–23

slide design, 116–117, 170
  backgrounds, 119

charts, 119–120, 170

composition and layout, 116–127, 170

images of people, 125–127, 170

Rule of Thirds, 120–124, 170

text, 116–119, 170

slide presentation, 127–129

speech structure, 25–32

supporting evidence, 135–136, 143–144, 171–173

square breathing, 8, 163

T

transitions, 26, 45, 166

V

visual aids, 21–22, 41, 111–130, 169–170
  audio, 41, 50, 115, 166, 169
  document cameras, 115, 169
  flip charts, 115, 169
  handouts, 23, 115, 169
  objects, 80, 112–114, 169
  overhead transparencies, 115, 169
  photographs, 115, 123, 126, 169
  props, 80, 112–114, 169
  slideware, 20, 21, 49, 108–109, 115–130, 169–170
  video, 115
  white boards, 21, 115, 169

vocal variety, 93–95, 168
  pause, 94–95, 168
  pitch, 94–95, 98, 168

vocal warmup, 95–96

W

wedding toasts, 159, 160–161, 171